Organization of
Public Schools

D. RICHARD WYNN, *1918-*

Associate Dean
School of Education
University of Pittsburgh

The Center for Applied Research in Education, Inc.
Washington, D.C.

LB
2805
.W9

Foreword

This volume of the Library of Education Series although small, justifies its title. It is particularly noteworthy for excellent selection of content. Research is brought to bear when it is applicable; otherwise, professional experience in educational administration is the source of its material. It should be useful to those who seek a bird's eye view of the field—both as to current conditions and emerging issues and trends.

The book begins by describing the relation of that uniquely American institution—the local school district—to the state and federal levels of government. The various forms which local school districts take are indicated, and their strengths and weaknesses are pointed out. Attention is given the factors contributing to the continuing reorganization of local school districts, factors and procedures which must be taken into account if greater effectiveness is to be achieved by agencies of government.

The volume then deals with arrangements for local control and administration of education. The origin and evolution of the role of boards of education are succinctly described, as are evolving arrangements for the administration and supervision of school systems.

The various forms of attendance unit, at both the elementary and secondary school levels, are examined. Dogmatism is avoided in dealing with such moot questions as vertical vs. horizontal organization of the administrative and supervisory staff, team teaching, the selfcontained vs. the departmentally organized classroom, and heterogeneous vs. homogeneous grouping.

The chapter devoted to trends and issues in school organization and staffing is most interesting. Most of the live issues in this field are identified and with few exceptions are dealt with in a judicious manner.

Organization of Public Schools should be useful especially to the

v

beginning student of education and to the layman anxious to survey the major issues and trends of this dynamic field. Even experienced administrators will find it interesting. I did.

JOHN K. NORTON
Professor Emeritus
Teachers College
Columbia University

Contents

Organization of
Public Schools

CHAPTER I

Organization of the School District

The School District in Relation
to State and Federal Government

One of the unique characteristics of public education in the United States is the tradition of strong local control. This tradition arose very early and has been zealously guarded throughout the history of the nation. During the Colonial period, most schools were privately controlled, and supported largely by tuition fees. Some schools were church supported; they were usually organized to serve charity students. Education in the Colonies was, as it had been for centuries abroad, a luxury available to those who could afford it or a charity available to those not too proud to accept it.

But after the Revolution, demand arose for new means of school support and control. The architects of the young republic recognized that education was essential to informed voting. Washington, Jefferson, Madison, and later Horace Mann, among many others, insisted that popular government could not survive without popular enlightenment. Education could no longer be regarded as a private luxury; rather it had become a public necessity. If education was to become a privilege enjoyed by all, it had to be made universal; if it was to be universal, it had to be free; if it had to be free, it would have to be publicly supported. Thus began the long and bitterly contested struggle for free universal public education and the rise of the common school, one of the most significant and distinctive chronicles in American history.

The concept of public control of education was practically implicit in the concept of public support, although some religious denominations argued for church control. Inevitably it was decided that public control must follow public support lest sectarian interests impose their particular doctrines on the students. Should this control be exercised by federal, state, or local government? The tradition of local control of schools was already strong in the New

1

England states by the time of the Revolution. Local control was a natural consequence in a sparsely settled nation that was largely rural, but decentralized authority over education was significant for another reason. Many of the colonists had emigrated to the New World to escape the tyranny imposed by the strong central governments of Europe. And, the more for having just undergone a struggle for independence from one of those powers, the nation's founders were understandably wary of the centralization of power, particularly power over education. Education is not specifically mentioned in the Constitution. By the Tenth Amendment, which reserves to the states powers not specifically restricted to the federal government nor denied the states, control over education is a state matter.

But the question of whether state governments or local communities should control education went long unsettled. Some people insisted that control of education was a fundamental prerogative of parents and local communities and that, therefore, state control would be invasion of local self-government. Horace Mann, Henry Barnard, and others insisted that only state control could enforce satisfactory standards and distribute financial support in such a way as to insure equal educational opportunity for all, regardless of local variations in wealth and effort. Despite sporadic objections, the latter view prevailed, and eventually all states established constitutional provisions for systems of free public education. Although details of such provisions vary among the states, a state's legislature determines the organization and administration of the state's schools under a general mandate of the state constitution reinforced by the courts. The Constitution of Hawaii, for example, provides that

> The State shall provide for the establishment, support, and control of a statewide system of public schools free from sectarian control, a state university, public libraries and such other educational institutions as may be deemed desirable, including physical facilities therefor. There shall be no segregation in public educational institutions because of race, religion or ancestry; nor shall public funds be appropriated for the support or benefit of any sectarian or private educational institution.

Thus, control of education is a legal function in which each state exercises plenary power over its schools. The fifty state systems of education vary widely in points of policy and program. Most states delegate to their local school districts much of the responsibility for the operation of schools within the framework of general state policy for education.

Under the "common defense and general welfare" clause of the Constitution (Art. I, Sec. 8), the federal government exercises its interest in education in a variety of ways. The Supreme Court guards against educational practices that violate the Constitution. The executive branch of the federal government acts principally through the United States Office of Education; that agency renders many important services, such as research and consultation. The Congress has enacted many laws providing financial support for various aspects of education. Nevertheless, the federal government exercises far less control and influence over education than do the governments of most other countries of the world.[1]

The Nature of the School District

Education, like any public service, requires an administrative structure. Although states have plenary power to organize public education in any manner they wish, every state has created school districts of various types. These school districts are the heart of the administrative structure and the locus of much of the operational control of the schools delegated by the state.

Legally, the school district is regarded as a quasi-corporation, a creature of the state, rather than as a municipal corporation. A municipal corporation operates primarily from local interest and advantage; it is established to assist the locality in administering its local concerns. A quasi-corporation is an instrument established by a state to execute state policy. Since the school district is a creation of the state, and since the state has plenary power over education, the school district exists at the pleasure of the state. A state may create, abolish, or alter school districts subject only to such limitations as may be provided in the state constitution. Courts have generally held that school districts have those powers specifically granted them by the legislature as well as those powers which can be reasonably implied or essential to carrying out statutory grants.

---

[1] For a more complete discussion of the role and function of governments in education see other volumes in the Library of Education series.

Advantages and Disadvantages
of Local Control

No other nation places as much responsibility for the operation of schools in the hands of local school districts as does the United States. Local control of education is regarded as a vital safeguard of our liberties. There are presently nearly 35,000 local boards of education. As long as much of the control of schools rests with them, it will be impossible for vested interests to gain control of any large sector of public instruction as a means of disseminating their particular doctrines. Concern that schools be independent of political control has resulted in school districts that, in most communities except large cities, are virtually autonomous governmental units, existing separate and independent of municipal government. Thus, control of education is generally regarded as unique among the functions of government.

Local control of education tends to encourage active public interest in education. Because control of education is close to the people, they tend to exercise this control more vigorously than if it rested at the state or federal level. As a result, people's interest in education and their expectations of schools tend to be raised.

Another advantage claimed for decentralized school control is increased capacity of schools to respond to unique local needs. Schools subject to local control can be more flexible, more immediately responsive, than they could be under a highly centralized structure. One of the great strengths of American education is diversity, a great variety of indigenous educational systems uniquely responsive to needs that vary in time and differ from place to place. This flexibility of educational policy derived from decentralized control also encourages creativity and experimentation, the handmaidens of educational progress.

The disadvantages of a decentralized educational system are reciprocals of its advantages. The great diversity in education results in disparities of scope and quality, and therefore, extreme disparities in educational opportunity. In one state a child may find free public junior colleges readily available, but in other states no such institutions exist. If through local control schools are readily responsive to local needs, it is possible that they will be less responsive to common national needs than were they more centralized. Many thoughtful persons insist there is urgent need for a national advisory body on education to establish recommended standards and indicate the direction in which education must develop to satisfy our national purposes more directly than is now the case.

Types of School Districts

Figure 1 reveals the various types of school districts which prevail in the several states.

State districts. Hawaii has only one school district for the entire state, typifying the purest form of state district. Alaska School District One, geographically the largest school district in the nation, contains all the schools of the state except for those in a number of cities and villages where some control of education is vested locally in city councils. No local boards of education exist in Alaska. Thus Alaska is really a combination of state and local districts.

County units. Nevada and Utah and most states east of the Mis-

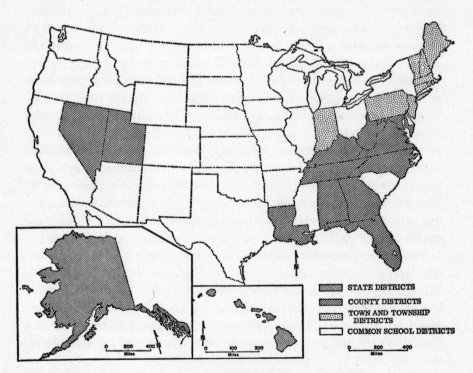

STATE DISTRICTS
COUNTY DISTRICTS
TOWN AND TOWNSHIP DISTRICTS
COMMON SCHOOL DISTRICTS

Figure 1. Types of School Districts in Each State.

sissippi and south of the Ohio River are organized on the county unit plan. The county has traditionally been a strong unit of government in most of these states and it was natural that the county should become the operational unit for education. Some of the states have consolidated their local districts into county units. The county provides a convenient if often arbitrary basis for the consolidation of a number of school systems into larger administrative units. In most of the other states of the nation, a county office of education exists as an intermediate office between the state and the local school districts.[2] But in the states mentioned above the county is the actual operating unit, usually for both the elementary and secondary schools of the county. In those states, schools are under the administrative control of a county board of education and a county superintendent of schools appointed by the board in some states, elected by the people in others. In county units of organization, the functions of the county board and superintendent are respectively similar to those of the local board and superintendent in states with local school districts. The county school unit is nearly always organized apart from, and is usually fiscally independent of, the country's general government. Where a city is contained within a county but is not coextensive with it, the city is included in the county school unit in some states, but in other states the city may be organized as an autonomous administrative unit within the county unit. County units vary greatly in size but most of them are large enough to offer a modern educational program at a reasonable per-pupil cost.

Town and township units. Many school districts in the New England states, New Jersey, Pennsylvania, and Indiana and some school districts in Wisconsin, Iowa, and Michigan are organized on a town and township basis. In Illinois, township school districts are organized for secondary school purposes only. In New England, the political unit called a "town" usually comprises a coherent village and the rural area surrounding it—a much more natural community and a more logical school unit than are most of what are called "townships" in other states. In New Jersey, Pennsylvania, and Indiana, many city, town, or borough school districts exist within township boundaries. Many of the smaller town and township districts that are too small to offer efficient school programs are being

---

[2] See other volumes in the Library of Education series for a more complete discussion of the role and function of the intermediate office in education.

joined with other towns or townships to form larger school units.

Common school district units.   In most of the western states and in New York, Ohio, Michigan, South Carolina, and Mississippi, the common school district is the local school unit. In rural areas particularly these districts tend to be quite small. Sometimes they operate one-teacher schools; sometimes they operate no schools at all, sending their students to other districts on a tuition basis. Very often district boundaries were established through early surveys, sometimes along lines of latitude or longitude, rivers, Indian trails, highways, or other such landmarks that have little relationship to natural community boundaries or logical school system organization. Common school districts are usually not coextensive with other geopolitical units. In some states, district boundaries have been gerrymandered for political reasons into irregular shapes producing quite grotesque school districts.

The common school district was established as a neighborhood institution to meet the simple educational needs of small rural settlements in an agrarian society. It served these needs well and became deeply involved as a focal point of the loyalties, customs, and values of rural life. But as communities grew larger and life more complex, the common school district became increasingly obsolescent. Unable to meet the more complex educational needs of an industrializing society, the common school districts either sent their children to larger school systems, merged with other common school districts, or continued to operate outmoded educational programs. In some states, particularly New York, significant progress has been made in the reorganization of these districts into more sensible patterns of larger school units.

City units.   In many states large cities operate their own school systems independently of the district, township, or county in which they lie. Large city school districts frequently present unique problems of school organization and control, requiring special legislation applicable to them solely. For example, boards of education are appointed in more than half the city districts, rather than elected, as they are in most other districts. City districts are often subject to special provisions or limitations with respect to school finance and state aid. Review of the school budget and control of the school tax rate by municipal authorities are fairly common in large city school districts, particularly in those cities where the board of education is

appointed. The boundaries of city school districts are not always coextensive with the boundaries of the municipality. Some states have
enacted legislation permitting city school districts to annex contiguous areas.

Regional districts.   Several states, particularly New Jersey, New
York, Illinois, and California, enable local districts to combine to
form a regional high school district while operating their elementary
schools separately. Most other states have followed the usually more
desirable practice of combining districts for both elementary and
secondary education, thereby tending to insure greater articulation
and continuity of the educational program.

Reorganization of School Districts

A great many school districts in the United States are too small
or too poorly organized to offer adequate educational programs economically and efficiently. Most authorities on education believe a
school district should have adequate wealth and population, be congruent with a natural community, and be independent of municipal
government in order to function adequately.

Size.   Despite striking progress in the reorganization of school
districts over the last several decades, a great many small schools
still remain. About one district in five is still too small to operate
any schools of its own; more than a quarter of the nation's school
districts still enroll fewer than fifty pupils each; over 20,000 one-
room schools remain in operation; about half of the school districts
do not operate high schools. Despite their great number, small
school districts serve only a very small proportion of the total school
population. For example, although nearly 20 per cent of the public
schools in the United States are one-teacher schools, their teaching
staffs collectively represent only 2 per cent of all classroom teachers.

A school district ought to be large enough to provide adequate
basic educational opportunity at reasonable cost. Definitions of
"adequate" size vary. A study by the Institute of Administrative
Research at Teachers College, Columbia University, concluded that
the population size of a school system was significantly related to
school quality. The study showed that school systems in communities of 20,000 to 50,000 population have the optimum conditions
for promoting school quality. As school communities become larger

than 50,000 or smaller than 20,000, conditions become less favorable to the promotion of school quality.[3] The White House Conference on Education concluded that 1,200 students is the minimal enrollment required for efficiency in a local unit, and that gains in efficiency could be expected with increases in enrollment up to 10,000. Pennsylvania has recently stipulated that all school districts must reorganize to form units of not less than 4000 pupils, except that in sparsely populated areas of the state units having a minimum student population of 2,500 in Grades 1–12 are required. Conant concluded that an adequate high school program is not possible with a graduating class of less than 100, which would suggest a minimum total school enrollment, Grades 1–12, of about 1,500. It is estimated that less than 10 per cent of the current school districts could meet this minimum specification, some indication of what remains to be accomplished in school district reorganization. Perhaps the pre-eminent dilemma in school district reorganization is how to secure a school district that is large enough to provide adequate and efficient education, yet small enough to retain a sense of community identification.

School districts also vary greatly in geographic area—some school districts are larger than some states. Most of the school districts of very large area are located in the sparsely populated regions of the West; often they contain more square miles than pupils. There are also many school districts, particularly in the Midwest, that are quite small both in area and enrollment.

Wealth. A school district should be large enough to include sufficient wealth. Districts vary greatly in per-pupil wealth, commonly by as much as 20 to 1. Although small districts are not necessarily poor and large districts not necessarily wealthy, the per-pupil wealth of a district tends to be greater in larger school districts. Many small districts have a taxable wealth that is grossly inadequate to support of adequate educational programs even though enrollments may be large enough to make modern school programs feasible. School district reorganization tends to pool the taxable wealth of the combined districts, evening out, to some extent, great disparities among contiguous smaller districts' abilities to support modern edu-

[3] Arthur D. Swanson, "Relations between Community Size and School Quality," *Research Bulletin*, Vol. 2, No. 1 (New York: Institute of Administrative Research, Teachers College, Columbia University, October, 1961).

cational programs. Large school systems also tend to reduce per-pupil costs by providing more economical organization, more equitable distribution of revenues, and more equitable local tax burdens. However, reorganized districts rarely reduce over-all expenditures because the expanded and enriched educational program which normally follows entails greater total costs. There is little agreement on what constitutes an "adequate" level of wealth. One rule of thumb suggests that the true valuation per child of school age should be at least $25,000. A reasonable tax from that base, plus state and federal aid, would yield enough revenue to support a fairly adequate educational program. Obviously, the pattern of state and federal aid available would influence this factor.

Natural community.   Ideally, a school district should comprise a cohesive community including those people held together by common economic, social, and cultural interests and activities. For example, a small city, its suburbs, and their surrounding rural areas are bound together by natural terrain, transportation, and trade, civic, recreational, and cultural characteristics constituting a natural school-community. In such instances educational needs and expectations are likely to be more compatible with community interests than they are in more heterogeneous communities, and schools are less likely to suffer from cleavages which arise in arbitrarily defined geographic areas having little community coherence. Many districts satisfy the natural-community criterion fairly well.

School district boundaries established a century or more ago along rivers and highways and trails very often fail to preserve natural communities. School district boundaries sometimes bisect communities. A village may be constituted a town school system, but its surrounding natural environs may be constituted a separate township school district. Township schoolbuses may transport pupils living on one side of the township directly past a town school to another school on the other side of the township.

School district reorganization was once regarded as primarily a rural problem. However, urbanization of our society has resulted in the rapid rise of city school districts and the growth of suburban districts surrounding the city. These urban-suburban complexes have created new problems of school district reorganization. City boundaries drawn years ago are usually too narrow to include all that grew to be a natural metropolitan area. In many respects a city and its suburbs are one, yet obsolete city school district boundaries often separate available school buildings from pupils and much taxable wealth from areas where it is most needed. Economic forces may precipitate a scramble among urban and suburban areas for financial advantage. Poorer districts seek to join the wealthier, but the latter hold out against them. Neighboring suburbs compete with each other to annex land having valuable industrial potential. With explosive force and speed urban and suburban growth overruns areas that were formerly rural, paying no attention to school district lines, swallowing up villages and townships, merging them into an amorphous mass. Large housing developments often create big new enrollments without producing comparable taxable wealth, overwhelming available school facilities and creating severe financial burden. When school buildings cannot be built fast enough, double —sometimes triple—sessions result. Lacking social and economic cohesion, the rural structure of school and municipal organization persisting in newly developed suburbs is frequently not adequate to the new task set it.

These problems are sometimes solved by extension of municipal boundaries, annexation by a city of neighboring areas, or merger of a central city with its surrounding area into a single school district. Forward-looking regional planning anticipating these problems fosters the most helpful solutions to them. School redistricting laws specifically designed for the reorganization of sparsely settled, stable rural areas frequently do not well serve the needs of heavily populated, rapidly-changing suburban and metropolitan areas.

Within large cities, unique problems arise out of sheer size of districts. For example, only eight states enroll more pupils than the New York City school district; nine of the largest city school systems enroll more students than the total public school enrollment in each of the seven least populous states. Our modern enormous cities are amorphous masses of humanity having little community identification. As middle- and upper-class families flee cities for the suburbs, they are replaced by families of low socioeconomic status, often newly arrived from underprivileged rural areas. Mobility of school populations is high. Urban redevelopment, even in the most energetic metropolis, can hardly keep pace with the growth of slums. Segregated housing leads to *de facto* school segregation in northern cities as well as southern. This condition, along with the

generally inferior schools found in slum areas, precipitates demands
for school integration which can usually be accomplished only by
transporting children from schools in their own neighborhoods to
schools in other parts of the city. These circumstances among others
prevent the adoption of natural, coherent communities as a basis for
school organization in large metropolises. Some cities, notably Chicago and Atlanta, have moved toward a more decentralized organization with the creation of school system subdivisions in the hope
that schools may become better oriented toward subcommunities
within the larger metropolis. Many of the problems of large-city
school districts appear almost insoluble.

Independent of municipal government. A school district
should be separate from municipal government. The rationale for
separation derives from the unique function of education in American democracy. Sound government depends upon an informed citi-
zenry. If education were subject to partisan political influence, there
could be no assurance of fair, objective treatment of social, political,
and economic problems in the school curriculum. If management
of schools were subservient to municipal authority, there would be
no assurance that a state's plenary power over education could be
exercised. If a board of education is to assume responsibility for the
welfare of a school system, it must have control over the determination and administration of the school budget. Such independence is
essential if boards of education are to discharge their responsibilities
to all the people, free of partisan political consideration in such
matters as the selection of staff, determination of the curriculum,
levy of taxes, and expenditure of funds.

The prevailing policy in the United States has provided for local
administration of schools independently of other municipal functions through the agency of autonomous local boards of education.
Litigations involving these matters have generally sustained the policy—the exceptions occur most commonly in cities where municipal
authorities sometimes appoint the board of education, levy school
taxes, and control the budget. In some cases they even exercise authority directly or indirectly over the selection of school personnel
and the content of the curriculum. There have been cases in which
municipal authority over education has been exercised wisely, but
education has generally suffered where it has been associated with
city government.

An adequate educational program. The ultimate test of a school district's adequacy lies in its ability to maintain a program sufficient in scope and quality to meet the educational needs of its clientele. A school district able to attract and retain a competent faculty, employ capable administrative and supervisory personnel in sufficient number, offer an educational program that enables students to become worthy members of society, satisfy a wide variety of student interests and abilities, provide adequate buildings and instructional materials, and maintain effective relations with the community is an adequate school district.

Reorganization in progress. Because many school districts fail to meet the tests of adequacy, there has been widespread movement toward the reorganization [4] of school districts into larger units. Although school districts were being reorganized in some states more than a century ago, the greatest progress in reorganization has taken place since World War II. Since 1945 the number of school districts in the United States has been reduced by two-thirds, from 103,000 to about 35,000. Although some district reorganization has taken place in most states, progress has been phenomenal in some but slow in others. Nevada, for example, reduced the number of its districts from 196 to 17 by changing from the common school district to the county unit. South Dakota, on the other hand, had 3400 districts at the close of World War II and 3100 in 1960. Despite the remarkable progress accomplished in many states, much remains to be done. As noted earlier, a great many districts are still too small or too poorly organized to provide basic educational programs at reasonable cost.

Procedures of reorganization. The responsibility for improving school district organization lies with state legislatures constitutionally invested with plenary powers over education, including the powers to create, destroy, or alter school districts. All states have enacted legislation relating to the organization and reorganization of school districts. This legislation can be classified into three general categories: mandatory, permissive, and mandatory planning with local option.

---

[4] The term *consolidation* is sometimes used synonymously with *reorganization.* More precisely, *consolidation* refers to the combination of small schools or attendance areas within the same district into larger school units; *reorganization,* to the merger of several school districts or administrative units into a single larger district.

Most of the mandatory provisions have provided for direct reorganization by state action. Ten states have by legislative action abolished existing local school districts and established the county as the school unit. Five states have enacted mandatory legislation delegating authority for school district reorganization to county and state agencies without approval of the electorate. In some states, however, county boards of education are required to submit plans for reorganization for approval by the state board of education. In a few cases state legislation grants full authority to a county agency to reorganize school districts by direct action. In 22 states mandatory legislation has forced abolition of only such districts as are below a certain size. This type of legislation usually delegates to county or state agencies authorization to combine small districts with adjoining districts.

Permissive legislation grants local districts the right to merge on their own initiative with other districts. Approximately three-fourths of the states [5] have enacted this type of legislation. In most states these permissive arrangements for merging school districts do not require the approval of the county or state educational authority. Action is usually initiated by a petition signed by a stated number or percentage of electors, or by action proposed by local school boards and put for approval to the electorate through a referendum. In most instances of permissive legislation, no provision is made for over-all planning of school district reorganization. Some states have miscellaneous laws incorporating provisions relative to the merger of districts of different sizes. Some of the permissive plans offer financial advantages in the form of increased state aid to reorganized districts.

Some states have been reluctant to mandate reorganization yet disinclined to endure the slow progress which often results from complete reliance upon local initiative. Fifteen states have enacted laws which mandate planning for reorganization but also retain some permissive aspects. Such legislation provides for statewide or countywide plans for reorganization based upon local studies of school needs and resources. The chief state school officer, state board of education, or state committee is charged with responsibility for counseling, reviewing, and approving or disapproving reor-

---

[5] The number of states cited exceeds 50 because many states have several different types of legislation for different sizes or classes of school districts.

ganization plans. The actual plans are usually prepared by the county board of education, or by a county committee which holds hearings on proposed plans and then puts them to a referendum.

An essential feature of the permissive and mandatory planning-local option procedures is the requirement of approval by the local electorate. Success in achieving approval of the mandatory planning-local option procedure seems to depend upon the inclusion of provisions for financial incentives and reimbursement for increased transportation costs, legal provision for handling combined assets and liabilities, alternate plans in the event the first plan is rejected by the voters, and deadlines for the completion of reorganization plans and elections.

In general, the states which have made the most rapid progress in school district reorganization have been those with mandatory legislation or some combination of mandatory and permissive legislation. Mandatory legislation has the obvious advantage of getting the job done quickly. It is criticized by some on the grounds that it pre-empts local prerogatives and undermines democratic local control of education. On the other hand, it is argued that, since education is a legal function of the state, it is entirely proper for the state through its elected legislature to handle the reorganization of districts by direct legislative action. When responsibility for drawing redistricting plans is delegated to state and county agencies with provisions for careful study and hearings, greater opportunity is provided for flexibility to meet unique local needs and circumstances.

The major advantage of permissive legislation is its provision for greater exercise of public opinion with respect to local reorganization patterns. Presumably the local option feature permits voters to accept or reject a reorganization plan on the basis of its merits. In reality, the local option arrangement frequently delays needed reorganization because people are often slow to recognize the need for reorganization; reluctant to abandon local autonomy in the control of schools; fearful of losing community identity; concerned about pupil transportation, increased costs, or possible inequities arising out of merged debts, facilities, and tax rates. The solution calls for enough mandate to secure forthright and responsible action but sufficient permissiveness to insure sound adaptation of reorganization plans to meet the unique expectations and resources of the people.

A study by the American Association of School Administrators suggested the following principles and practices should be observed in the development of statewide programs of school district reorganization:

1. The legislature should make or cause to be made a comprehensive study of the state school system and existing school laws as a basis for developing and enacting a new district reorganization law.

2. Existing laws which would hinder, retard, or prevent the new legislation from working should be amended or repealed. Laws which permit haphazard merging of districts during the time of reorganization or that tend to perpetuate small districts with financial rewards should be carefully scrutinized.

3. The new legislation should be simple, clear, and concise, with provisions that make reorganization possible without unnecessary disturbance and confusion.

4. Adequate financial support for state and local agencies, for commissions, for committees, and for other groups charged with responsibility for studying, planning, and carrying on a reorganization program is most desirable.

5. Laws which clearly define and fix responsibilities intended to be placed at the state level and responsibilities intended to be placed at the local level reduce confusion and disputes. Insofar as possible, vagueness and indefiniteness should be avoided.

6. It is desirable to create at the state level a committee or commission of five to nine members, closely identified with the state department of education to assume important reorganization responsibilities. . . .

7. A committee of five to nine members should be established at the county level. . . . This county committee should be regarded as a permanent reorganization agency that will assume leadership for the reorganization of school districts until the job is fairly well completed. . . .

8. Adequate state equalization funds for current school operations are essential to successful programs of school district reorganization. . . .

9. The method of distributing state funds should not encourage the retention of unnecessarily small school districts. . . .

10. The method of distributing state school funds should offer incentives to adequate school district organization. . . .

11. The state should provide aid for paying the cost of pupil transportation, capital outlay, retirement of bonded indebtedness incurred prior to reorganization, educational services for exceptional children and adult education. . . .

12. State subsidies for tuition of nonresident pupils should be available only as a last resort and in cases of unavoidable necessity. . . .[6]

---

[6] American Association of School Administrators, *School District Organization* (Washington, D.C.: The Association, 1958), pp. 202–203; 239–44.

Advantages and disadvantages of reorganization.   Reorganization of school districts usually makes possible the extension and enrichment of the educational program. The curriculum is typically broadened to include new courses of study. Kindergartens, high schools, junior colleges, and adult education programs often become feasible in larger administrative units. Specialized personnel in guidance, health, supervision, and administration can be provided, and specialized facilities such as libraries, gymnasiums, shops, and health rooms become more commonly available as enrollment increases. Several studies indicate that students from larger high schools tend to be more successful in college than students from small high schools. The tax base is usually broadened, resulting in more equitable distribution of school support. That, plus the increase in school enrollment, usually results in more efficient use of the tax dollar.

However, the reorganization of local school districts may create new problems. As districts become larger, the locus of school control may be further removed from the people, making a close relationship between the community and the school difficult to maintain. But in most instances the advantages of reorganization have far outweighed the disadvantages. Despite the progress already made, much remains to be accomplished—indeed, the reorganization of school districts must be regarded as a continuous process in most states.

CHAPTER II

Administrative Organization and Staffing
of School Systems

The administrative structure of school systems typically includes a board of education which exercises legislative and judicial functions, and an administrator (in larger districts, an administrative staff) who exercises the executive function. Some school districts are still too small to employ an administrator.

Boards of Education

Historical development. The early public schools in New England were commonly governed by town meetings or by the selectmen of the town. As communities grew larger and the administration of schools became more complex, school committees were appointed from among the selectmen to manage the schools. In some New England communities the school governing body is still designated the "school committee"; in other localities it is variously designated the "board of education," "school board," "board of school directors," "board of school trustees," or "board of school commissioners." In this discussion, the term *board of education* will be used to designate any board of control of public schools.

In 1826 Massachusetts passed a law authorizing the establishment of school committees, separate from and independent of municipal governing bodies, to have "general charge and superintendence of all the public schools." This law is often regarded as the official legal beginning of the board of education. In the early nineteenth century, before the advent of the professional school administrator, boards of education performed both legislative and executive functions. They established school policy and managed the schools as well; they hired, paid, and even supervised teachers on occasion; they purchased supplies and equipment and approved the curriculum and methods of teaching. Very often individual board members were assigned almost unilateral jurisdiction over individual buildings in certain geographic areas of the school district—each member to the building in the ward in which he lived and which he represented on the board. Small wonder that these officials sometimes came to be known as "school directors," a title which persists in some states. As the educational operation grew larger and more complex, particularly in cities, more and more persons were elected or appointed to the board of education. In some cities and towns each ward or other subdivision constituted its own school district with its own school board. Philadelphia at one time had more than 500 school directors. This fragmentation of school organization into many districts within the same city and the parcelling out of school control to impossibly large numbers of school directors was obviously unsound.

By mid-nineteenth century, three significant reforms were under way in many cities. First, the consolidation of city ward school units into a single citywide district resulted in greater equalization of educational opportunity and financial burden and in more efficient use of school funds and facilities. Second, cumbersome boards of education were reduced in number to one member from each ward or original school district; eventually, ward representation was eliminated altogether. Third, the need for full-time, chief local school administrators was recognized, and officials called "superintendents" were increasingly employed in the latter half of the nineteenth century. At first, only minor executive functions were relinquished to the superintendent, or supervising principal, but gradually many of the major administrative functions of the school system were delegated to him and his staff. However, legal accountability for most administrative acts continued to rest with the board of education. Thus the chief school administrator became the executive officer of the board of education, exercising administrative authority delegated to him by the board.

Legal status and powers. The local school district is a quasi-corporation created by the state. The board of education is the administrative body and the legal agent of the school district. The board is vested by law with the authority and responsibility necessary for the conduct of education in the district. The legal powers of the board of education are essentially those of the school district.

Boards of education have in general those powers which are expressly granted by statute as well as those powers implied by or essential to the exercise of the powers expressly granted. This concept of the power of boards of education is deeply rooted in statutes and judicial opinion. When a school system, acting under the authority of an implied power of its board of education, undertakes some educational innovation upon which the statutes are silent, the legitimacy of the power may be challenged in litigation. The court must decide whether the presumed enabling power is properly an implied power of the board. In general, courts have been fairly liberal in their interpretation of properly implied powers, particularly when such powers are apparently necessary educationally and when boards have acted in good faith. The cause of educational progress has been aided significantly by such liberality. In some instances, of course, courts have been forced to rule that certain practices are indeed beyond the reasonably implied powers of boards of education.

The board of education exercises authority only as a corporate body; board members cannot exercise the corporate authority individually. The board cannot divest itself of authority granted it by the legislature. Although boards can and do delegate ministerial tasks to committees of the board and to the school administrator and his staff, the board must review and approve actions and recommendations before they can legally take effect.

In general, the board of education exercises legislative and judicial functions of the school district and delegates to the school administrator and his staff most of the executive or ministerial functions. Many of the judicial functions of the board call for the exercise of discretionary powers not always prescribed specifically by law. The courts have generally been liberal in their judgment regarding the propriety of exercise of such powers. They are not inclined to rule upon the wisdom of discretionary decisions as long as there is no evidence of injustice, capriciousness, fraud, malice, or bad faith.

The specific powers of boards of education vary widely from state to state; often, within a state, large school districts enjoy powers denied smaller ones. In general these powers include the right to establish rules and regulations governing the operation of schools; to enter into contracts and other agreements; to determine the school curriculum and approve courses of study; to set the length of the school term; to employ personnel and set the conditions of their employment; to acquire sites for construction and equip school buildings; to establish the school budget, borrow money, and determine revenue. In all cases the board of education must exercise these rights within the limitations established by law. For examples, the board of education may employ teachers, but it can employ only those teachers who meet certification requirements established by the state; a board of education may borrow money, but it may borrow only to the limit set by state law and in accordance with procedures prescribed by law.

Selection and appointment of board members. In most school districts, local board of education members are elected by the people on a nonpartisan basis, often at special school elections held apart from general political elections. Membership by appointment is most common in large cities; the larger the city, the likelier this method of selection. Board members are appointed in more than half of the city districts of over 500,000 population. Appointment is usually made by the city council or similar legislative body, the mayor, the courts, or judges, in that order of frequency.

The case for election of board members is supported by the following arguments:

An elected board is more responsive to the will of the people, and therefore more democratic.

Elected boards, particularly those elected on a nonpartisan basis, are less likely to feel beholden to a particular official or body or special interest group.

Election of boards of education stimulates greater public interest in schools.

The case for the appointment of board members is supported by these arguments:

Many of the best candidates will accept appointment to the board of education but are reluctant to submit themselves to the ordeal of campaigning for the position, particularly if partisan campaigning is required.

The appointing authority can be held fully accountable to the people for the quality of the board's service. Many political scientists believe that the mayor ought to be held clearly accountable for all city government responsibilities, including schools, but he could not be held accountable for an elected board of education.

Although quality of boards varies whether they are appointed or elected, the majority of responsible opinion clearly favors election of board members on a nonpartisan basis.

Qualifications and characteristics of board members. The magnitude and importance of the educational enterprise require that school board members be selected carefully. The legal requirements for membership most commonly specified by law include residency in the school district and minimum age of 21. Legal stipulations aside, a school board member should have a genuine interest in school affairs; be openminded and willing to subordinate self-interests; be able to give time and energy to the office; be reasonably well educated; have an understanding of the community; possess skill in working with people; and be representative of the community at large rather than partisan to a particular area, religion, political party, or special interest group. Studies of the composition of city school boards indicate that members come largely from business and professional groups and are generally representative of a narrow socioeconomic segment of the community. They are usually better educated than the general adult population. Their private income is generally above the average for their community. Fewer than one in seven city board members are women.

Term of office. The term of office for school board members commonly ranges between three and six years. New members require time to become familiar with the school system and its problems and the educational needs of the community. Several studies indicate that a school board member's effectiveness generally increases with term in office. For this reason, terms of office should be fairly long and promising board members encouraged to serve successive terms. Terms of office should overlap to avoid majority turnover of board membership during a short period of time.

Organization and operation. The vast majority of school boards contain five to nine members. The number is usually specified by law. Large cities sometimes have more than nine members; small school systems, fewer than five. In general, five to nine members is considered an ideal size—large enough to get the work done with dispatch as a committee of the whole, yet small enough to permit free discussion.

The laws of most states specify that an annual organization meeting of the board of education be held on a specified date for the purpose of electing officers and conducting other organizational business. Except in a few large cities, where the mayor is ex officio chairman of the board, the chairman or president and vice-chairman or vice-president of the board are elected by the board of education from among its own membership. In some school districts the chairmanship is rotated automatically among the board members.

Great variation of practice exists with respect to the offices of secretary and treasurer of boards of education. In a growing number of school systems the superintendent, either by statutory provision or by board regulation, serves as secretary of the school district. When that is the case, much of the routine work of the secretaryship is usually delegated to the superintendent's secretarial staff. In a few instances, the business manager of the school system serves also as secretary of the board of education, a practice not generally considered desirable.

A board may elect either a member or nonmember treasurer. In the larger school systems, the board secretaryship, or "clerk of the board" as the office is sometimes designated, is usually a full-time job that is often held by a nonmember. In those smaller school systems in which the secretaryship is not a full-time job, a member of the board is frequently elected to the office. In some instances the county or city treasurer serves as treasurer to the board of education. Although board of education members commonly serve without salary, secretaries and treasurers are usually paid for their services because the volume of work required by these offices is too much to impose on volunteers. Boards of education employ special staff assistance such as school attorneys, architects, and auditors, as needed, and usually on a part-time basis in smaller districts.

When school boards consisted of many members and operated without the services of a professional school administrator, standing committees were necessary. The tradition of the standing committee still persists, particularly in city school systems, although its incidence is steadily declining. Most contemporary standing committees are used to perform administrative tasks, study problems, and advise the board. It is argued that they save the time of the full board and make for more efficient operation. However, expert opinion is to the contrary. A system of standing committees in effect divides the board into sub-boards which tend to discharge the board's functions piecemeal, and committees sometimes give only superficial consideration to their responsibilities. If the entire board reviews fully the recommendations of the committees, no time is saved; if the full board does not review the work of the committees, the responsibility of the board may be diluted. Very often, the responsibilities of the various committees are not well defined, resulting in uncoordinated efforts. Moreover, the functions which they perform —fact-finding, advisement of the board, the handling of executive tasks—are often more germane to the school's professional staff.

Many boards have made effective use of special committees and a committee of the whole. Unlike standing committees, which are permanent and continuing, special committees are assigned a particular task and cease to exist when the task is completed. The committee of the whole is an informal, unofficial assembly of the full board convened to assess problems, gather facts, and consider action, often in meetings unattended by the public. Formal action may be taken subsequently in an official meeting of the board.

Most boards of education hold regular monthly meetings, although some meet bi-monthly. Meetings are sometimes suspended during the summer months, particularly in smaller districts. A school board has the right to transact business only in duly constituted board meetings. The time, place, and date of regular meetings should be publicized by the board of education. Special meetings are necessary on occasion and should be called by the board president or chairman according to procedure authorized by law or by board regulations. Board meetings should be convened promptly, follow a carefully prepared agenda in harmony with an established order of business, be conducted according to standard rules of parliamentary procedure, and facilitate full discussion of issues without waste of time. Actions of the board, including roll call votes on important matters, should be carefully recorded and the minutes of the board should be regarded as public documents.

Some states require that, with certain exceptions, board of education meetings be open to the public. The conduct of the affairs of the public school system is public business, and therefore should ordinarily be open to public scrutiny and public participation. This is a necessary safeguard against dishonest or unjust board action. Board meetings should make provision for orderly presentation by the public of questions or testimony on matters of interest to either individuals or groups in attendance. Public attendance and participation in board of education meetings should be not only permitted but also encouraged. However, a board of education is entirely justified to meet on certain occasions in executive session, from which public and press are excluded. This prerogative should not be abused to suit the convenience of the board or to withhold from the public information to which it is entitled. Private sessions of the board should be called when the discussion of private matters relating to an individual employee, pupil, or parent is necessary. A board of education may also meet in executive session when it is considering the acquisition of land or property—public knowledge of such proposals might result in an inflation of price.

The primary functions of the board of education are legislative in nature. The board, with the advisement of the superintendent and his staff, establishes the policies and regulations which guide the school system in its operation. One of the most reliable hallmarks of a good board of education is the care with which it establishes and maintains policy. A policy is a statement of principle to be used as a guide in making decisions with respect to the general operation of the schools. Matters of policy are enacted from time to time at meetings of the board. They should be codified periodically into comprehensive policy statements widely available to board members, employees, and the public. Well-conceived policy statements tend to insure consistency of action, facilitate orientation of new board members and school personnel, protect the board of education and administration from waste of time in having to consider each individual case, enhance the possibility of fair play and equal treatment for all, protect the board somewhat from charges of unfairness and pleas for preferential treatment, and reduce uncertainty and indecision. The formulation of a policy statement is also a useful exercise in clarifying the school system's purposes and philosophy and translating them into a *modus operandi*. School policy should be developed cooperatively with the superintendent and professional staff, should be broad and general in nature, and should be reviewed and brought up to date periodically. There is considerable evidence to indicate that those boards of education that operate under carefully prepared policy statements are generally more effective than those which proceed without such policy definition.[1]

The responsibility for the execution of policy should be delegated to the superintendent of schools and his staff. The superintendent

---

[1] Maurice E. Stapley, *School Board Studies* (Chicago: Midwest Administration Center, University of Chicago, 1957), p. 3.

of schools, as noted earlier, is the executive officer of the board. Good organization requires clear differentiation between the executive functions of the professional administrators of the school system and the legislative or policy-making functions of the board of education. However, in practice it is sometimes difficult to draw clearly the line between legislative and executive functions. The board's rules, regulations, and adopted policies can help to make the distinction clear. Perhaps the most important single responsibility of the board of education is to employ a competent superintendent of schools to whom responsibility for the good administration of the school system can be delegated with confidence. Board members should refrain from invading the administrator's prerogatives, but should hold him fully accountable and require him to submit periodic reports as a basis for evaluating the administration of the school. If the board of education lacks confidence in the superintendent's competency, proper relief lies in replacing him rather than in pre-empting his responsibilities.

The relationship between the board of education and its executive officer ought to be defined as clearly as possible through policy statements and through a job description of the position of the chief administrator. Although the board of education has final legal authority over such matters as employment of personnel and approval of the curriculum, it should act in these matters only upon recommendation of the superintendent. For example, the superintendent should nominate for employment candidates for all professional and nonprofessional positions; the board of education should hire only those persons who have been thus recommended. If the board cannot accept the recommendations presented, it should request the superintendent to prepare new recommendations rather than substitute choices of its own. Similarly, action relating to matters of curriculum, teaching processes, materials and supplies, and organization of classes and schools should originate with the executive officer of the board and his staff. Indeed, as the professionally prepared expert on education, the superintendent should be expected to render his professional advice to the board on practically all matters confronting it, particularly those which have major consequence with respect to the education of children and youth.

Another major responsibility of the board of education is the maintenance of good relations with the community. The high degree of local control of education built into the structure of schools in the United States is based in part upon the belief that education should be responsive to the unique needs of the particular community the school serves. This is possible only when the board of education successfully maintains interaction with the community. Administration of public schools is a vital public trust. It cannot be fully realized without the sanction of the public. A public that is poorly informed or rarely consulted is not in position to function wisely. As indicated earlier, wise boards of education encourage public attendance and participation at board meetings. Good school systems engage in a continuous effort to keep the public informed on education progress and problems through a straightforward program of public relations. Indeed, there is clear evidence that the level of public understanding of education is related to the quality of education which prevails in any community.[2]

A recent phenomenon in American education is the renaissance of public interest in education. One manifestation of this development has been the dramatic rise of lay advisory committees and councils, sometimes known as school community councils. A mere handful at the close of World War II, such committees and councils now exist in a great number of school districts in the country. Wise boards of education have encouraged their formation and sought their council. Practically all communities contain a variety of other organizations vitally interested in school operation, and cooperative relationships with them should be encouraged by boards of education. However, it must be emphasized that these organizations can serve only in an advisory relationship to the board. The board is without legal sanction to delegate or dilute any of its statutory authority over education to these groups.

Improving the effectiveness of boards of education. Many boards of education make intelligent use of outside professional advice, calling upon consultants from colleges and universities, state departments of education, and other professional groups for help with particular problems. Many school boards belong to state associations of school boards, all of which are affiliated with the National School Boards Association, an organization emerging as a powerful force in American public education. These associations

---

[2] Donald H. Ross, ed., *Administration for Adaptability* (New York: Metropolitan School Study Council, Teachers College, Columbia University, 1958), pp. 294–97.

carry on research, disseminate publications, and hold conferences and conventions aimed toward the improvement of school board operation. Some professional associations and universities conduct in-service training programs and institutes for school board members. A number of school systems may join with a university to form school study councils which conduct experimentation and research and accelerate the diffusion of good educational practices.

Much research has been undertaken recently to study the problem of school board effectiveness. One notable study concluded that some of the factors most closely related to the effective performance of boards of education are: the level of the board member's formal education, his skill in analyzing problems and making decisions, his ability to interpret educational problems to the community and capitalize upon its help, his willingness to subordinate personal interests, and his understanding of the distinction between the legislative and executive functions of the superintendent and board.[3]

Administrative and Supervisory Staff Organization

Historical development.   The earliest schools were one-teacher schools. School administration was simple, carried on largely by the teacher himself, subject to some review by the school committee or school directors. As communities grew larger, schools became multi-teacher units and one teacher was commonly designated as the "principal teacher" of the school building, hence the origin of the term *principal*. This principal teacher (or head teacher as he was sometimes called) was a full-time teacher with the additional responsibility, and sometimes additional pay, for the administration of the school. Thus the principal came into being long before the superintendent of schools.

As villages grew into cities and multibuilding school systems arose, there was increasing need for administrative services. At first, the function was attempted by school directors who assumed responsibility for schools in their jurisdiction. This part-time service by laymen proved inadequate. By mid-nineteenth century the chief local school administrator had begun to appear, particularly in the cities. The early prototype of this position, known as the "superin-

---

[3] Stapley, *op. cit.*, pp. 42–50.

tendent" or "supervising principal," handled functions that were largely clerical matters related to attendance, enrollment, and expenditures. The term *school management* was more commonly used than *school administration,* and is more descriptive of the fairly primitive level of operations which prevailed during the latter half of the nineteenth century. There were no real scholars of school administration and very little scientific study of the job.

By the beginning of the twentieth century, unmistakable signs of the professionalization of school administration began to appear. Schools of education introduced graduate courses in school administration. University professors conducted surveys of school systems, appraising educational practices and offering recommendations for improvement. These surveys are the beginning of the literature in school administration. The first professional association for school superintendents created was the Department of Superintendence of the National Education Association, the forerunner of the American Association of School Administrators, which today numbers approximately 15,000 members. Later, certification requirements for administrative positions were established by the states.

State and county superintendents of schools played an important part in the development of school administration, but with the emphasis upon decentralization of administrative control in America, the great surge of development has been at the local level, involving primarily superintendents of schools and principals.

As the administrative function became more complex, administrative staffs of larger school districts were increased by the addition of assistant superintendents, supervisors of instruction, business managers, curriculum directors, directors of buildings and grounds, and other specializations. Attention had to be given to the organization of this corps of administrators. Tables of organization and division of administrative responsibility became more commonplace.

By the early twentieth century new concepts of educational administration began to emerge. The earlier concepts of school administration, drawn largely from scientific management with its emphasis upon the impersonal components of administration, gradually gave way to a more sophisticated conceptualization of the job. As the broader relationship of the school with society became more discernible, the role of the school administrator was more frequently described as that of a "social engineer" or "educational statesman."

The interpersonal and cultural dimensions of school administration became better perceived, and concepts of "educational leadership" displaced older concepts of "school management." The social sciences were drawn upon more fully both in the preparation of school administrators and in the study of administrative problems. The Great Depression, World War II, and the cold war which followed it forced the school administrator out of his earlier narrow preoccupation with impersonal aspects of administration into a broader concern for social and moral aspects of educational leadership.

At mid-twentieth century several significant new forces emerged to help shape the destiny of educational administration. The W. K. Kellogg Foundation granted approximately $7 million, which was supplemented by funds from other sources, to support the Cooperative Program in Educational Administration and subsequent related enterprises. This program, centered in eight universities across the country, was designed to study educational administration and to improve administrative practice. It contributed substantially to the fund of research in school administration, advanced the formulation of theory, and brought the social sciences and other disciplines to bear more effectively upon the understanding and practice of school administration.[4]

Several major consequences of the Cooperative Program in Educational Administration (CPEA) are also worthy of mention. The cooperative relationships among university programs in school administration begun under the aegis of CPEA were formalized and extended under the University Council of Educational Administration, established in 1956. The Council unites the more eminent university programs in educational administration for cooperative action toward improved preparation of school administrators, inservice development of professors of educational administration, and the advancement and dissemination of relevant research. The Committee for the Advancement of School Administration, established in 1955 under the leadership of the American Association of School Administrators with a grant from the W. K. Kellogg Foundation, has sought to strengthen school administration by communicating research findings to practitioners, encouraging states to

---

[4] For more information about the influence of the CPEA, see Hollis A. Moore, Jr., *Studies in School Administration* (Washington, D.C.: American Association of School Administrators, 1957).

raise certification standards for administrators, upgrading the standards of accreditation pertaining to institutions preparing administrators, and improving the practices of boards of education in selecting administrators. Another noteworthy step in the improvement of educational administration was accomplished by vote of the American Association of School Administrators in raising its requirements for membership to include completion of a two-year program of graduate study in an accredited program.

These and other forces have combined to accelerate the improvement of educational administration since 1950—no other period has seen such rapid and significant advances in educational administration. Among the more notable consequences have been increased rigor in the recruitment and selection of persons for preparation in school administration; stronger preparation programs that provide more depth in the study of administration and more breadth in the social sciences particularly; improved methods of instruction, including internships and other kinds of field or laboratory experiences; and greater recognition of the importance of theory and research in school administration.

Status of the school administrator. The legal status of the school administrator lacks clear definition in many states. Usually the superintendent of schools is regarded as the executive officer of the board of education and an ex officio nonvoting member of the board. He is also the chief professional advisor to the board of education. Some of his responsibilities are defined by law, others by the rules and regulations of the local board of education. In most states superintendents of schools have no legal tenure, serving relatively short terms at the pleasure of the board of education. The school principal, unlike the superintendent of schools, usually has tenure and cannot be dismissed except for reasons specified by law.

The superintendent of schools is the educational leader of the school's professional staff as well as the executive officer of the board of education. These two roles embody some degree of role conflict and sometimes give rise to incompatible expectations on the part of the public, board of education, faculty, and students. Moreover, the school administrator is part of an interrelated chain of command that extends from the school building to the statehouse, and beyond. The school principal has general responsibility for the administration of a school building, what is sometimes referred to as an "attendance area." But the school principal administers his school under the general jurisdiction of the superintendent of schools and within limitations set by local rules and regulations. The local superintendent of schools may also be accountable in some matters to the county or state superintendent of schools.

Because of the close relationship of the schools to the public, school administrators often work closely with various community agencies both public and private. The decisions of school administrators are often shaped either directly or indirectly from forces and values of the local, state, national, or international communities. Thus, school administration operates within a complex field of forces, legally, politically, geographically, and socially.[5] The discussion which follows draws attention exclusively to the internal administrative organization of school systems and the educational programs they offer.

Purpose and importance of organization. Organization is typically regarded as the first step in the administrative process. It is a necessary and primary function of administration, regardless of the size or nature of the enterprise. The purpose of organization is to clarify and distribute responsibility and authority among individuals and groups in an orderly manner consistent with the purposes of the institution. Organization is, then, an attempt to accomplish the purposes of an institution through an established division of labor and responsibility. If organization is to be effective and efficient, these institutional purposes must be clearly defined and understood. Organization, by the foregoing definition, is an effort to arrange an orderly and efficient distribution of authority and responsibility. This permits specialization of function through subdivision of tasks and also permits the fixing of accountability. This characteristic of organization suggests the importance of job descriptions and organization charts as means of making the distribution of authority and responsibility explicit and orderly. The definition also suggests that organization is a dynamic and continuous process of maintaining a pattern of working relations among individuals and groups. It integrates their activities so that maximum contribution can be made toward the institution's goals with a minimum of energy. Also, it is

---

[5] For a fuller discussion of this broader context in which school administration must operate, see Roald F. Campbell and Russell T. Gregg, eds., *Administrative Behavior in Education* (New York: Harper & Row, Publishers, 1957), Chap. 2.

clear from the definition that organization is not an end in itself, but a means whereby the purposes of the institution are achieved.

The importance of good organization is readily apparent—when it exists, things get done efficiently. People understand the metes and bounds of their authority. They know what to do and to whom to report. Changes are accomplished smoothly and emergencies are infrequent or nonexistent. When good organization does not exist, one frequently hears people complain: "But I got different instructions from him." "There's too much paper-pushing." "I never found out what happened." "I didn't know who was responsible for it." "No one told me." "You should have sent it to *me*."

Nevertheless, many school systems operate with obsolete or poorly designed administrative structures.[6] In many cases a severe numerical inadequacy in the administrative staff has resulted from its failure to keep pace with the more rapid growth of the school system. In other cases, the administrative organization has grown "Topsy-like"—new positions, sometimes poorly defined, are added indiscriminately without relevance to other components of the organization. Some administrators have not recognized the importance of efficient organization, insisting that it is necessary only to hire good people, that they will make their own jobs and work out their own organizational arrangements. Building an administrative staff without a well thought out system of organization is probably as indefensible as buying school supplies without specifications or handling school revenues and expenditures without a budget.

Guidelines to administrative organization. Griffiths and associates have established these six guidelines of organization: [7]

1. The role of the administrative staff in an institution is to create an organization within which the decision-making process can operate effectively. The organization should permit decisions to be made as close to the source of effective action as possible.

2. The administrative staff of an educational institution should be organized to provide individual staff members with as much freedom for initiative as is consistent with efficient operation and prudential controls.

---

[6] Cooperative Development of Public School Administration, *Your Schools and Staffing: Current Practice in Administrative Staffing in New York State* (Albany, N.Y.: CDPSA, 1955), pp. 15–16.

[7] Daniel E. Griffiths, David L. Clark, D. Richard Wynn, and Laurence Iannaccone, *Organizing Schools for Effective Education* (Danville, Ill.; The Interstate Printers and Publishers, 1962), pp. 71–72.

Hierarchical levels should be added to the organization with caution, and only when deemed imperative to maintain reasonable control over the institution.

3. The administrative functions and the sources of decision-making in an institution should be organized to provide machinery for democratic operation and decentralized decision-making.

4. The purpose of organization is to clarify and distribute responsibility and authority among individuals and groups in an orderly fashion consistent with the purposes of the institution. The structure of the institution is determined by the nature of its decision-making process and the organization of the institution should be established to provide for the most effective operation of this process.

5. An institution should be organized with a unitary source of decision-making at its head. Authority and responsibility delegated by the chief administrator should result in a unitary pattern of decision-making levels among all subordinates in the institution.

6. The administrative organization, by its very structure, should provide for the continuous and cooperative evaluation and redirection of the organization from the standpoint of adequacy (the degree to which goals are reached) and efficiency (the degree to which goals are reached relative to the available resources).

These guidelines place emphasis on the following concepts of organization:

A broad span of control
A flat organization
The building unit as the basis of organization
The specialist as a staff officer
A decentralized organization
The purpose of the institution as the primary criterion for organization
Unitary control and supervision

Numerical adequacy of specialized personnel. A persistent problem confronting many school systems is the determination and justification of an adequate administrative and supervisory staff. One study sought to illuminate this problem by observing the work load of school specialists, analyzing the recommendations of professional associations and other agencies that have given thought to the problem of reasonable work loads in their particular fields of interest. The study warns that the following criteria should be regarded as general guides to administrative staffing adequacy, because needs vary according to the individual school organization and adaptations should be made to accommodate local variables.

TABLE I

SUGGESTED MINIMUM NUMBER OF FULL-TIME ADMINISTRATORS AND SUPERVISORS PER STUDENT IN AVERAGE DAILY MEMBERSHIP *

Number of pupils in average daily membership	Minimum number of administrators and supervisors
1000–1199	5–7
1200–1399	6–8
1400–1599	7–9
1600–1799	8–10
1800–1999	9–11
2000–2199	9–12
2200–2399	10–13
2400–2599	11–14
2600–2799	12–15
2800–2999	13–16
3000–3499	14–18
3500–3999	16–22
4000–4999	18–25

* Richard Wynn, *Guides to the Solution of Administrative Staffing Problems* (Danville, Ill.: The Interstate Printers and Publishers, 1958), p. 8.

The study recommended the following minimums with respect to other specialists: [8]

GENERAL

Adult Education

2000–3000 students in adult school: one half-time director
For each adult school of over 3000: one full-time director
For each additional 1000 students: one additional half-time assistant

Attendance

1500–2000 students: one full-time director of attendance
For each additional 1500–2000: one additional visiting teacher

Specialists in special education

For each 2000 students, approximately:
One half-time specialist in instruction of physically handicapped
One half-time specialist in instruction of the partially sighted
One half-time speech correctionist
One half-time to two full-time specialists in instruction of the gifted and mentally handicapped
One quarter-time specialist in instruction of the homebound

---

[8] Adapted from Richard Wynn, *Guides to the Solution of Administrative Staffing Problems* (Danville, Ill.: The Interstate Printers and Publishers, 1958), pp. 9–10.

Health Services

For each 2000 students, approximately:
One half-time physician or equivalent
One half-time dentist or equivalent
One half-time to two full-time nurses
Two full-time dental hygienists
One half-time psychologist

ELEMENTARY

(Based on elementary attendance units housing enrollments of 350–450)
One full-time principal
One secretary-clerk
One librarian
One cafeteria manager
Fourteen–twenty teachers
Two–four helping teachers

SECONDARY

(Based on secondary attendance units housing enrollments of 800–1200)
One principal
One–two assistant principals
Three–four office personnel
One librarian
One cafeteria manager
One nurse
Two–three guidance counselors
One–two art teachers
One–three music teachers
Two–four homemaking teachers
Two–four industrial arts teachers
Thirty-five–fifty other teachers as needed

Prototypes of administrative organization of school districts.
An examination of several actual patterns of administrative structure may be helpful in visualizing the operational relationships and functions of the various components of a school system's administrative organization. Each administrative structure must be adapted to the unique needs and resources of a particular school system. Therefore there are almost as many different administrative organizations as there are school systems in the United States. As would be expected, the larger the school system, the larger and more complex its administrative structure.

In the very smallest school districts there may be no administrative organization other than a board of education administering a faculty of but one or several teachers. Slightly larger districts typically employ a superintendent of schools or supervising principal who is alone responsible for all of the administrative functions performed in the district. As districts become still larger, principalships are established next. Figure 2 illustrates the most common administrative organization prevailing in smaller school districts. In organizations of this type, the superintendent is typically a full-time administrator, although the principals—particularly the elementary principals—may be part-time administrators as well as part-time teachers. If there are several small elementary schools in the district, a full-time elementary principal may serve several of the schools in that capacity. In small school organizations, lines of authority are uncomplicated, communication easy, interpersonal rela-

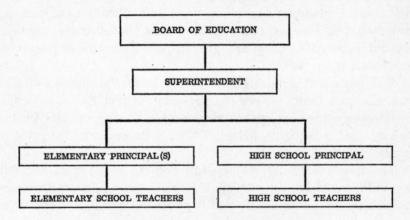

Figure 2. Organization of Small School District

tions among administrators and teachers simple and informal. Working relationships evolve empirically, and job descriptions are rarely made explicit.

Figure 3 illustrates the administrative organization of "Ridgeway," a fictional school district of moderate size.[9] Ridgeway is a

9 This description is adapted from Griffiths, et al., Chap. 6. This source contains six case descriptions of administrative organizations of school systems of various sizes and characters.

relatively stable community of 25,000 population. It has a school population of 4200 pupils attending six elementary schools, one junior and one senior high school. The professional staff—teachers, supervisors, and administrators—numbers 196.

The chief administrator in Ridgeway is called the "superintendent of education," rather than the traditional "superintendent of schools." Ridgeway likes to think of him as the coordinator of, or at least consultant to, all the educational agencies of the community, instead of just the schools. Two assistant superintendents, one for educational opportunity and the other for funds and facilities, a coordinator of research, and an administrative intern report directly to the superintendent. In addition to these central office staff members, building principals are directly responsible to the superintendent.

The assistant superintendent for educational opportunity has three coordinators reporting to him—coordinators of pupil personnel services, instructional services, and adult education and community relations. The assistant superintendent for funds and facilities has a director of buildings and grounds and a director of food services reporting to him.

Staff personnel reporting to coordinators in the division of educational opportunity include the physician, dentist, dental hygienist, audiometer technician, speech correctionist, visiting teachers, nurses, special-area consultants, helping teachers, counselors, and psychologists.

The assignment of an administrative intern to the superintendent is a unique and worthy practice. Under this arrangement, Ridgeway cooperates with a university that is preparing graduate students for school administration.

The principals, with the assistant superintendents, the director of research, the director of adult education, the administrative intern, and the superintendent, comprise what is known in Ridgeway as the "administrative cabinet." The cabinet, which meets weekly, is an open forum in which questions are raised and problems discussed. At any given meeting, one or more of the coordinators, with resource persons from the staff, may meet with the cabinet to discuss problems which directly relate to their fields of specialization.

The administrative cabinet serves several important functions. First, it provides systematic opportunity for wider participation in

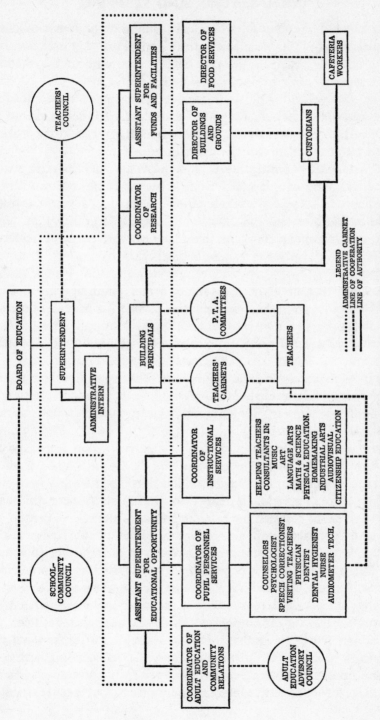

Figure 3. Administrative Organization of Ridgeway Schools

BOARD OF EDUCATION

SUPERINTENDENT

ADMINISTRATIVE INTERN

TEACHERS' COUNCIL

SCHOOL-COMMUNITY COUNCIL

ASSISTANT SUPERINTENDENT FOR FUNDS AND FACILITIES

DIRECTOR OF FOOD SERVICES

DIRECTOR OF BUILDINGS AND GROUNDS

CAFETERIA WORKERS

CUSTODIANS

COORDINATOR OF RESEARCH

BUILDING PRINCIPALS

P. T. A. COMMITTEES

TEACHERS' CABINETS

TEACHERS

COORDINATOR OF INSTRUCTIONAL SERVICES

HELPING TEACHERS CONSULTANTS IN:
MUSIC
ART
LANGUAGE ARTS
MATH & SCIENCE
PHYSICAL EDUCATION,
HOMEMAKING
INDUSTRIAL ARTS
AUDIOVISUAL
CITIZENSHIP EDUCATION

ASSISTANT SUPERINTENDENT FOR EDUCATIONAL OPPORTUNITY

COORDINATOR OF PUPIL PERSONNEL SERVICES

COUNSELORS
PSYCHOLOGIST
SPEECH CORRECTIONIST
VISITING TEACHERS
PHYSICIAN
DENTIST
DENTAL HYGIENIST
NURSE
AUDIOMETER TECH.

COORDINATOR OF ADULT EDUCATION AND COMMUNITY RELATIONS

ADULT EDUCATION ADVISORY COUNCIL

LEGEND
.... ADMINISTRATIVE CABINET
- - - - - LINE OF COOPERATION
———— LINE OF AUTHORITY

decision-making. The superintendent confides that he would not venture a major decision without the counsel of this group.

Second, the cabinet is an excellent communications medium through which, for example, principals can report problems, programs, and needs to the central office. The superintendent can report and interpret school board problems and decisions to the administrative staff. The director of research can report the findings of his latest study on teacher selection practices.

Third, the administrative cabinet provides an important means of coordinating program and policy. For example, the problem of whether Ridgeway can tolerate cursive writing in some first grades and manuscript writing in others can be resolved in the cabinet. The problems of coordination and budgeting effort, frequently neglected in human enterprises, are greatly facilitated by the administrative cabinet.

Fourth, the functions of evaluation and planning can be managed better through the administrative cabinet. It provides time and opportunity to contemplate and anticipate long-range problems of real consequence. It provides a means for gathering more substantial data and judging the efficiency of programs and practices.

Ridgeway recognizes the importance of research in school administration and has employed the services of a coordinator of research. He functions as a staff officer and is responsible to the superintendent.

A joint school-community council created several years ago has proved an effective means of involving Ridgeway's lay citizens in school and community problems. The purposes of the school-community council are clearly defined in its charter. A clear distinction has been made between the responsibilities of the school-community council, the function of which is primarily that of studying problems and giving advice, and the responsibilities of the board of education, the function of which is primarily that of legislating school district policy. The council consists of twenty-five members who serve overlapping three-year terms. The committee meets monthly and operates from an agenda prepared by its executive committee. The superintendent believes that it is very desirable for professional staff members and lay people to work together in such organizations. The presence of staff members, who are in a position to give the council facts relative to problems under discussion, is quite essential.

The presence of staff members also helps the council to distinguish between matters of broad social policy—a proper prerogative of the council—and matters of professional or technical concern—an improper prerogative of the council. Moreover, better school-community rapport tends to result from the interaction of lay and professional people.

The PTA committees, noted on the organizational chart, exist in each school. Each committee emphasizes study and action projects of particular interest to its school community. Each committee has a representative on the school-community council.

In addition to these media of school-community interaction, Ridgeway utilizes a wide variety of special reports, brochures, bulletins, news releases, and radio programs for communicating with the general public. Although the superintendent gives considerable time to the development of good school-community relations, as any good superintendent must, he nevertheless delegates much of the actual work to the coordinator of adult education and community relations. This is a natural combination of functions, since management of the adult education program and of community relations bring this person into wide contact with lay persons and groups. The coordinator has an adult education advisory council at his service for help in the development of the adult education program.

Primary responsibility for the administration of the educational program rests with the assistant superintendent for educational opportunity, although a great many persons assist him in this function. In a more traditional organization, he would have reporting to him a director of health and physical education, a music supervisor, perhaps a director of elementary education, and so on. Not so in Ridgeway. Three coordinators—one of adult education and community relations, whose function has already been described, one of pupil personnel services, and one of instructional services—report to him. Responsible to the coordinator of pupil personnel services are counselors, a psychologist, a speech correctionist, visiting teachers, the school physician, the school dentist, the dental hygienist, nurses, and other specialists. Responsible to the coordinator of instructional services are the helping teachers and consultants in music, art, language arts, mathematics, science, physical education, homemaking, industrial arts, citizenship education, audiovisual education, and so on. These personnel are thought of as a corps of master teachers assigned to service at the school system level. They work very closely with the beginning teachers.

This school system views administrative and supervisory personnel as the service arms of the classroom. With the exception of the superintendent, all central office personnel are staff officers working primarily on an on-call basis. The assistant superintendent and the coordinators have continuing responsibility for scheduling the consultants and providing leadership in the improvement of their fields of specialization. This relationship is shown as a "line of responsibility" in the organization (Figure 3). These helping teachers, consultants, and others have a line relationship with their respective coordinators and with the assistant superintendent for educational opportunity, inasmuch as they are personnel on the staff of the assistant superintendent and his coordinators. However, in the working operation of this organization, a teacher who needs help in, say, selection of curriculum materials would call upon the coordinator of instructional services to provide consultant service. While fulfilling this need, the coordinator and/or consultant are in effect working with the teacher and are, of course, under the authority of the building principal involved. This relationship with the principal is shown as a "line of cooperation" in Figure 3. Their relationship with the teacher is shown as a line of cooperation. Thus, these consultants are *supervised* in the technical aspects of their work by their coordinators but are *responsible* to the principal of the building in which they are working.

This arrangement leaves a principal in the preferred position of responsibility and accountability for the entire educational program of his school. In a more traditional organization, he may be superseded by a hierarchy of subject matter supervisors responsible for vertical segments of the program, leaving him with little more than the housekeeping details of management. However, integrity of program and accountability for results are not likely to obtain in high degree under that arrangement; moreover, teachers feel they are frequently working for two or more bosses.

Ridgeway's arrangement calls for principals who are educators as well as administrators. It calls for principals who can assume general responsibility for the total educational program of their respective schools as well as help formulate policy for the entire system, since they are also members of the system's administrative cabinet. The arrangement calls for broader training and wider understanding than many principals command. In Ridgeway, they rank but one level below the chief administrator, a level that in more traditional organizations would be occupied by an array of subject matter supervisors, assistant superintendents, directors, and others.

Ridgeway's organization is a manifestation of the flat organization discussed earlier. It provides administrative units having a high degree of autonomy, a greater freedom to adapt to the unique needs of the neighborhood which the particular school serves. It gives each school the right to be different. It encourages creativity and experimentation. Most important of all, it provides for integrity of program and accountability for results in each school—two characteristics typically lacking in tall organizations.

In the Ridgeway organization, administration of staff is shared between the central office and the building principal. If the building principal is to be accountable for the educational program in his school, obviously he must have a large share in selecting and assigning his staff, providing for their in-service development, and managing their supervision. However, salary scheduling, tenure, retirement, sick leave, and other benefits are administered through the central office.

Each principal works with his own teachers' cabinet, consisting of members elected from and by his faculty. Each school's cabinet considers problems of staff welfare, program improvement, community relations, and budget development for that particular school. Teachers' cabinets in each building serve a role on the building unit level corresponding to that of the administrative cabinet on the system level.

The superintendent, too, has a teachers' council, comprised of elected teacher representatives from each building and from each major subject division. The membership is rotated annually to give more people an opportunity to serve, and to distribute the burden of this type of service. This council meets monthly with the superintendent to deal primarily with personnel and instructional problems facing the system as a whole.

Ridgeway's superintendent retains final responsibility for the budget and plant, particularly with respect to major recommendations to the board. But he delegates a large measure of operating responsibility to the assistant superintendent for funds and facilities, a member of the administrative cabinet reporting to the superintendent. The coordinator of food services provides certain types of direct assistance to the school cafeterias. A coordinator of buildings and grounds, who has a strong background in plant maintenance and management, reports directly to this assistant superintendent. However, in harmony with Ridgeway's concept of the relatively autonomous school, the individual building principal rather than the coordinator of buildings and grounds makes recommendations to the superintendent regarding hiring, promoting, and dismissing custodians. The coordinator, however, cooperates with, or advises, the principal in screening applicants, managing their in-service training, and supervising their work, particularly in its technical phases. Similarly, the general operation of the school cafeterias is the responsibility of the building principal, although the coordinator of food services is responsible for planning menus, purchasing food and equipment, and carrying out other technical duties.

In the development of the budget, the principals, with the assistance of their teachers' cabinets and the assistant superintendent for funds and facilities, develop first drafts of the budgets for their individual buildings. These budgets are brought to the administrative cabinet where they are amalgamated into an over-all budget for the system. Necessary adjustments are hammered out in this cabinet. If subsequent adjustments must be made for individual buildings, budgets are taken back and worked over by the teachers' cabinets. This process is repeated until all budgets are compatible. Much of the detail of his operation is handled by the assistant superintendent for funds and facilities, who considers himself the servant rather than the master of the administrative cabinet in this regard. He holds the point of view that the budget is the financial plan which gives meaning to the educational plan. He recognizes that the development of the educational plan is the proper prerogative of the building principals and other cabinet members.

Informal Organization

It was once believed that if one understood the formal organization of a school system he understood how it really worked. But it has become increasingly evident that people often don't behave according to the specifications of the formal organization. One must usually look behind the scenes of the formal organization to understand fully the dynamics and nuances of the real power structure in any human enterprise. Let us take a look at just one such aspect of the Ridgeway school system.

For many years the Ridgeway teachers expected the superintendent of schools to represent to the board of education their interests in improved salaries. The superintendent, particularly when he was new in the community, had only limited influence upon the board of education and the teachers felt that their interests were not well represented. A group of teachers, led by Mr. Andover, a helping teacher in physical education and assistant football coach, insisted that teachers' salaries would never be substantially improved until the Ridgeway Teachers' Association assumed a more militant position and represented the teachers' salary interests directly to the board of education. Very little persuasion was needed to obtain Andover's consent to run for the presidency of the Ridgeway Teachers' Association and to lead the fight for better salaries. Andover's position as a helping teacher brought him into frequent contact with teachers throughout the system. These contacts, along with the appeal of his platform—namely, the transformation of the Teachers' Association into a strong bargaining agent—returned Andover a strong winner in the race for the presidency. With the help of a well-organized salary committee and the general support of the faculty, a new salary schedule proposal with substantially increased minima and maxima was agreed upon by the teachers and presented directly to the board of education by Andover and his colleagues on the salary committee. The new salary schedule was adopted with minor modifications.

Several factors made it possible for Andover to accomplish for the teachers in one year what the superintendent had failed to accomplish in several. First, Andover was a native of Ridgeway, well known and widely respected by the teachers and citizens of the community alike. His strategic position vis-à-vis the teachers has already been noted. As assistant football coach he had made through the years many effective contacts with influential people in the community. For the preceding three years he had served also as chairman of the county committee of the political party in power in the community. His advice was always sought by the party caucus concerning nominees for the local board of education. These factors gave

Andover powerful leverage in negotiating with the board of education on the matter of improved salaries for teachers. Indeed, it was suggested by several knowledgeable people that some of his most effective bargaining took place with individual school board members outside of board meetings.

The salary victory won by the Ridgeway Teachers' Association catapulted Andover into even greater esteem among his colleagues. More and more often the board of education turned quietly to him for advice, particularly on matters involving personnel policy. Teachers discovered that major problems relating to conditions of employment, if taken to Andover, soon found their way onto the board of education's agenda. But if they were taken to the superintendent through the Teachers' Council, positive and effective action was much less likely to follow.

Belatedly, the superintendent recognized the rising influence of Andover in the decision-making machinery of the school system. He perceived that Andover's influence, at least so far, had been both effective and constructive. Indeed, Andover stood for many of the same reforms that the superintendent supported but that had eluded him until Andover's influence was exercised. Andover's integrity and his dedication to the improvement of the Ridgeway school were unquestionable. But his loyalty to the chain of command and his respect for channels were another matter, as far as the superintendent was concerned. The superintendent wondered whether the organization could stand this power rivalry and, if not, what he could do about it to secure his own influence within the formal power structure of the organization.

The anecdote described above illustrates one interesting and not uncommon manifestation of what is known as "informal organization," which can be defined as those extralegal interpersonal relationships that shape the decision-making processes and the power structure of an organization. The term *extralegal* is not to be confused with *illegal*—there is nothing at all illegal about teachers exercising power through duly elected officers of their associations directly with the board of education. *Extralegal* suggests only that there is no mandate for such procedure in the formal organizational structure and that these informal relationships exist beyond the formal or legal organization. The term *interpersonal relationships* suggests that informal organization is manifest in undefined associations of people rather than through formal, institutionalized relationships implicit in organization charts. The operational test of whether informal organization has affected the formal power structure hinges on whether or not the decision-making processes have been reshaped—as indeed they were in Ridgeway.

Far too little is known about informal organization. Few studies of informal organization of school systems have been completed and all of them are quite recent.[10] Informal organization serves to solve pressing problems which are impossible or difficult to solve through the official institutional framework. Informal organization provides a circumvention of the formally prescribed channels and methods of procedure; thus, informal organization may compensate for the inadequacies of the formal organization. Someone once observed, perhaps not entirely facetiously, that the surest way to destroy an army would be to insist that it operate always entirely "by the book"; that is, strictly according to its formal organization. Thus armies, like school systems and other forms of human enterprise, develop informal organizations to accomplish more quickly or more efficiently those tasks which members of the organization view as necessary or desirable. Informal organization can also be regarded as representing those interests or personal goals of individuals that conflict with the institution's goals, as those are represented by the formal structure.

From this discussion it is evident that informal organization is neither good nor bad per se. If one assumes, for example, that higher salaries for Ridgeway teachers were good, then Mr. Andover's exercise of the informal power structure toward this goal was desirable. Informal organization can be either subversive or supportive.

It is also clear that the formal and informal organizations are closely related to each other, each reacting to and being influenced by the other. Had the Teachers' Council, a part of the formal organization, successfully represented the teachers' problems to the superintendent, and had the superintendent been effective in helping the board solve those problems, the circumvention of the formal organization by the Ridgeway Teachers' Association would have been unnecessary. But once the superior effectiveness of the informal organization was demonstrated in this matter, the status of the

---

[10] For one such study, see *ibid.*, Chaps. 14–16.

Teachers' Council and the superintendent in the power structure could never be the same.

Our example illustrated how informal organization can accomplish objectives beyond the capacity of the formal organization. Informal organization can also have the opposite effect: that is, it can delay, modify, hamper, and even destroy efforts of the formal organization which appear undesirable to individuals who wield the power of the informal organization.

Leadership within the informal organization is related to the range of interaction open to persons within the formal organization. In our example, Mr. Andover's position as helping teacher within the formal organization offered him an extensive range of interaction with other teachers in the school system. It gave him a strategic position from which to operate as an opinion builder within the formal organization.

This suggests that the school administrator can manipulate the formal organization in such a way as to affect the operation of the informal organization. For example, the Ridgeway superintendent might have transferred Andover to another position affording less opportunity for him to interact with other teachers in the school system. Or the superintendent might have made Andover a member of the Teachers' Council. This would have given Andover a position from which he could operate in the formal organization. This might have modified the rise of Andover's influence in the informal power structure manifest in the Ridgeway Teachers' Association. The superintendent, although denied direct leadership of the informal organization, can to some degree reduce the effectiveness of the informal organization or dissipate the needs and forces that encourage it by manipulating the formal organization. Or, to state it more positively, the existence of informal organization may be regarded as symptomatic of the need for reorganization of the formal organization. Analysis of the informal organization may serve as a guide for the improvement of the formal structure. In a perfect state of affairs, institutional and individual goals are congruent and there is no need for informal organization. Very often informal groups become institutionalized in the formal organization after their relevance and competency have been established through informal operation.

Griffiths and his associates have established several generalizations concerning informal organization:

1. The school is an organization which has informal as well as formal aspects of behavior and systems of relationships.

2. The informal organization has a definite structure containing subdivisions which persist over time. In the case of the school, its basic structure continues with little change from one academic year to another.

3. The customary network of relationships—cliques, groups, pairs, and the like—comprising the informal organization of the school is related to the formal patterns of behavior and interaction mandated by the formal organization.

4. The systems of behavior and relationships in the formal organization complement, supplement, and modify the system of behavior prescribed by the formal organization. Which modifications are constructive of the school's purposes and which are destructive can be determined only after an examination of the particular case.

5. Formal and informal organizations alike are vehicles by which the goals of individuals are both satisfied and frustrated.

6. The informal organization provides a kind of proving ground on which limited conflicts and adjustments of interests as well as trial-and-error learning can take place with a minimum of disturbance to the operations of the total institution. The maximum use of these functions of informal organization will be invaluable to the administrator.[11]

---

[11] *Ibid.*, pp. 292–93.

CHAPTER III

Organization of the Attendance Unit

So far the book has centered upon the organization of school districts and the administrative organization of school systems. Attention is turned now upon the organization of attendance units within the school system. In those small school districts which operate only one school building, an attendance unit is coextensive with a school district; a single attendance unit comprises the entire school system. Larger school systems contain a number of attendance units, usually under the administration of a principal, and commonly housed in separate school buildings. Attendance units vary greatly in size and organization.

Organization by Grade Levels

Throughout the history of education in the United States no clear-cut distinction between the limits of elementary and secondary education has emerged. There has been general agreement that Grades 1–6 belong to the elementary school, Grades 9–12 to the secondary or high school. The uncertainty precipitates around Grades 7 and 8. In approximately a fourth of those school systems in the country which operate high schools, a 6–3–3 type organization prevails.[1] The larger the school system, the more likely it is to be organized on the 6–3–3 plan. Small school systems find the 6–3–3 plan uneconomical and are more frequently organized on the 8–4 plan. In the 6–3–3 plan, elementary schools contain Grades 1–6; the junior high school contains Grades 7, 8, and 9; the senior high school includes Grades 10, 11, and 12. Less than a fourth of the school dis-

---

[1] All the data cited in this paragraph are derived from a study of school organizations in communities of over 2500 population by the National Education Association, Research Division, *Operation of Separate Junior High School* (Washington, D.C.: The Association, December, 1960).

tricts are organized on the 8–4 plan, in which the first eight grades are contained in the elementary schools and the last four in the secondary schools. Approximately a fifth of the school systems are organized on the 6–2–4 plan, in which the junior high school includes only Grades 7 and 8, with Grade 9 included in the senior high school. About a fifth of the schools maintain a 6–6 plan, in which the upper six grades operate as one secondary unit with no distinction between the junior and senior high school levels. The remaining school systems operate under a variety of other patterns; 7–5, 6–3–3–2, 6–4–2, among others.

As school systems grow larger through expanded population and reorganization, there is a steady trend toward a six-year rather than an eight-year elementary level. The rationale for the six-year elementary school depends largely upon considerations of child growth and development. Since puberty is reached by most children between ages twelve and fourteen, a different school environment becomes appropriate for young people after the sixth grade. School systems which attach significance to the differences between early adolescence and late adolescence are disposed to make distinctions between junior high school and senior high school organization. However, variations in the maturation process are legion, and youngsters at various stages of development inescapably will be combined regardless of the type of school organization. The superiority of one type of organization over another has never been conclusively established by research evidence. In many communities factors other than child development and educational philosophy affect decisions concerning school organization. The availability of space in school buildings, the cost of school construction, state aid formulas, and other realities very often influence the choice.

An interesting innovation in the organization of schools has been the development, in a few communities, of separate attendance units for kindergarten and Grades 1–3. These units are sometimes called "neighborhood schools" because they are small enough to permit the establishment of one in each neighborhood, thereby requiring only short walking distances of very young children. Neighborhood schools usually exist as satellites of larger upper-grade elementary schools. This type of organization, known as 3–3–3–3, is not in widespread use.

Organization of Elementary Schools

Administrative organization. Approximately half the elementary schools in communities of over 2500 population are K–6; approximately a fourth are 1–6; approximately an eighth are K–8; approximately a twelfth are 1–8; the remainder are either K–3 or 1–3. Over the years the trend in organization has been toward the elementary school that ends with the sixth grade. The median enrollment of elementary schools under the jurisdiction of supervising principals is slightly over 500; the median number of teachers, slightly less than 20. Size of the elementary school tends to increase with size of the community.

The administrative organization of most elementary schools is quite simple. It consists commonly of the principal, some part-time staff specialists, teachers, and office and custodial personnel. Less than an eighth of the elementary schools employ assistant principals, approximately half of whom are employed only part-time. Table II shows the availability of resource personnel in elementary schools.

TABLE II

ELEMENTARY PRINCIPALS HAVING CERTAIN RESOURCE PERSONNEL AVAILABLE

RESOURCE PERSONNEL	FULL-TIME *Per Cent*	PART-TIME *Per Cent*	NOT AVAILABLE *Per Cent*
School nurse	7	85	8
Special teacher or supervisor of music, vocal and/or instrumental	13	78	9
Special teacher or supervisor of art	9	61	30
Special teacher or supervisor of physical education	11	52	37
General supervisor	8	55	37
Special teacher or supervisor of speech	3	58	39
Psychologist	2	54	44
Teacher of homebound	5	48	47
School physician	1	46	53
Visiting teacher or social worker	2	43	55
School librarian	9	29	62
School dentist	1	37	62
Special teacher or supervisor of reading	3	32	65
Assistant principal	7	6	87
Special teacher or supervisor of science	2	10	88

Department of Elementary School Principals, National Education Association, *The Elementary School Principalship*—A Research Study, 37th Yearbook (Washington, D.C.: The Association, 1958), p. 64.

Several studies have recommended that an elementary attendance area should make possible a school with at least one teacher per grade (with an enrollment of 300 pupils in each elementary school preferred) and require that elementary pupils walk no more than three-fourths of a mile or travel by bus no more than a half-hour each way.

Nursery schools.   Nursery schools were originated to care for the children of working mothers; often they were little more than child care centers. But today, in the realization of the importance of the early childhood years in human development, the great potential of the nursery school is more clearly seen. Modern nursery schools seek to stimulate and guide the growth of children through the highly formative pre-elementary years. Nursery school programs are very informal, consisting largely of storytelling, playing, singing, dancing, and other fun activities.

Public nursery schools are quite uncommon in the United States. Less than 5 per cent of the urban school systems operate nursery schools. Nursery schools are virtually nonexistent in nonurban districts. There is no apparent trend toward any sizeable increase in the number of publicly supported nursery schools although there has been a steady growth of private nursery schools sponsored usually by churches, welfare agencies, and private groups quite apart from the public school system. The dearth of nursery school programs in public school systems is striking in the light of the extreme importance of the earliest years of childhood in the development of the individual. The nursery school today occupies a marginal position just outside the public school system, somewhat similar to that held by the kindergarten for many years.

Kindergartens.   An increasing number of school systems are including kindergarten programs. Approximately 70 per cent of the urban school systems maintain kindergartens. Most kindergartens are found in school systems of over 2500 population. Despite the growth in kindergarten education, only about 50 per cent of the five-year-olds and 70 per cent of the six-year-olds are in school. Unlike nursery schools, most kindergartens are publicly supported, integral parts of the elementary school unit. The trend is clearly toward expansion of kindergarten education.

The most common age for admission to kindergarten is five. Although most states do not compel school attendance for five-year-olds, twenty states have included kindergarten in their minimum foundation programs.

The general aim of the kindergarten is to smooth the transition from the family setting to the school environment and to help children adjust to larger groups. Kindergarten programs are designed to promote the physical, mental, social, and emotional growth of the child and to stimulate readiness for the more formidable tasks of the first grade. Kindergartens help young children learn to care for themselves, to get along with others, to become interested in books and other forms of communication, to develop physical coordination, and to develop skill in self-expression.

Primary grades.   The first three grades of the elementary school usually constitute the primary division. Kindergarten is combined with the first three grades to form the kindergarten-primary unit. Language arts and numbers constitute the main substance of the primary curriculum, with particular emphasis upon reading. Music, art, and handicrafts are also commonly included in the primary curriculum. In recent years, social studies, science, and foreign language study have sometimes been introduced in the early grades. Class size is usually held somewhat smaller in primary grades than in the middle and upper elementary grades primarily because immature and beginning students require more individual attention. Most schools maintain a somewhat shorter school day for primary grades, usually five and a half hours or less. The self-contained classroom is practically universal in the primary grades.

Approximately a fifth of the school systems of the country have adopted some sort of primary unit embracing the first three elementary grades and perhaps the kindergarten. The primary unit seeks to bring better articulation and coherence to early elementary education by reducing disparities between grade levels. Many primary units have been ungraded; that is, grade lines have been obliterated entirely, and children are permitted to move through a period of three or four years without reference to promotion or retardation by grade. Sometimes the same teacher remains with the same group for more than one year to further their continuous progress.

Middle grades.   Reading is still the most important single curricular activity of the middle grades (usually Grades 4, 5, and 6), but the emphasis is now more heavily upon extensive and enriched reading than upon mastery of the mechanical skills. The fourth grade marks the beginning of serious study of many new subject fields in both the social and physical sciences. As in the primary grades, the social, emotional, and physical development of the pupil is stressed along with intellectual growth. For the middle grades the school day is typically somewhat longer, usually five and a half to six hours long—and longer in many communities. Many school systems have instituted voluntary summer school programs for the middle grades. Approximately half the schools practice some departmentalization along with the partially self-contained classroom in the middle grades. The trend in that direction has been quite marked during the past decade, but complete departmentalization of the middle grades is quite rare. Completely self-contained classrooms prevail in approximately a third of the schools. Class size is typically larger in the middle grades than in the primary ones.

Upper grades.   Where Grades 7 and 8 continue to exist as a part of elementary education, they are commonly regarded as the upper grades. Departmentalization is more common in the upper grades with about a third of the schools completely departmentalized and another third partially departmentalized. The school day is usually six hours or longer in the upper grades. The subject matter content of the curriculum is similar to that of the middle grades but more advanced in substance. There is a strong trend toward the introduction in the upper grades of substance such as general science and general mathematics, formerly offered first in the ninth grade. In most school systems, regardless of the form of organization, Grades 7 and 8 are viewed as a transitional level from the elementary school, which is predominantly child-centered, to the secondary school, which places greater emphasis upon subject matter.

Special classes and schools.   Most elementary schools are general-purpose schools; that is, they are designed to serve all pupils alike, without specialization of curricula or of facilities. However, many school systems offer special education classes for elementary pupils with mental, physical, social, or emotional handicaps or disabilities. These classes are invariably much smaller in size because of the increased burden of instruction. Grade levels are more commonly obscured in the special education classes which are staffed by teachers with advanced preparation for such work. These special classes—"opportunity classes," as they are sometimes called —present materials, content, and method adapted to the particular need of these atypical children. Different standards of achievement are expected of them. Special physical facilities are usually needed for physically handicapped children. Wherever feasible, these special classes are conducted as an integral part of the elementary school system. However, some city school systems maintain separate elementary schools for mentally retarded or physically handicapped students.

Organization of Secondary Schools

There is great disparity among recommendations with respect to the minimum size of secondary school attendance areas. Conant has recommended that each high school have a graduating class of at least 100 students. The American Association of School Administrators recommends that high schools should be so located that no student need walk more than two miles nor ride a bus for longer than one hour one way. A great many high school attendance areas fail to meet even these modest standards. More than half the high schools in the nation enroll fewer than 250 students, yet these small high schools serve only a small percentage of the total high school population. They are unable to offer an adequate educational program, incapable of attracting and holding enough well-qualified teachers and administrators, and unable to operate economically.

Figure 4 illustrates the most common organizational patterns of secondary schools. The traditional four-year high school has declined sharply in recent years. More than four-fifths of the seventh- and eighth-grade students are now attending some form of junior high school or combined junior-senior high school. The most common form of junior-senior high school combination is the 6–3–3 plan, followed closely by the 6–6 plan. In the latter plan, both the junior and senior high schools comprise the same attendance unit and are usually housed in the same school building under the administration of one principal. In any case the purposes and programs of the junior and senior high schools should be differentiated if the unique functions of each are to be served. Figure 4 also illustrates extensions of the secondary program upward to include two years of public junior college. This may take the form of a six-year organization comprising Grades 9–14, or two four-year units in sequence including Grades 7–10 in the lower secondary division and Grades

11–14 in the upper secondary division. But the most common arrangement by far is the two-year junior college as a distinct unit apart from the junior and senior high school units.

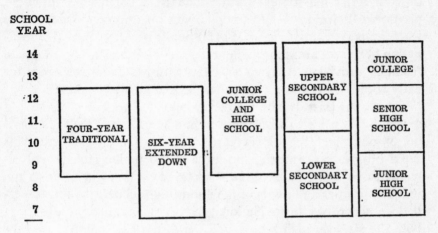

Figure 4. Organizational Patterns of Secondary Schools

Junior high schools.   The junior high school arose out of dissatisfaction with the 8–4 plan of organization, which too often failed to adapt to the unique needs of adolescents who are significantly different from both prepubescent and advanced teenage youth. Authorities argued that a distinct educational unit, the junior high school, was needed to serve properly the educational and other developmental needs of such youth. Ideally, according to the National Survey of Secondary Education, the junior high school should be characterized by flexibility in admission and promotion, programs of studies uniquely adapted to pre-adolescent youths, suitable extracurricular provisions, educational-vocational guidance services, special features for articulation between the elementary school and senior high school, a specially trained staff, and special housing and equipment. Various studies indicate that much remains to be done before these accommodations are widely realized.

In a recent study of the junior high school, Conant recommended minimum enrollments of at least 125 pupils in each of Grades 7 and 8 if they are part of a unified 6–6 system; a full-time guidance specialist for every 250–300 pupils in Grades 7 and 8; provision for smooth transition from the elementary to the secondary school;

provision of a separate three-year junior high school as part of a
6–3–3 organization if there are 750 or more pupils in Grades 7–9;
provision for a capable junior high school principal and a full-time
assistant principal for each 750 students; a balanced staff of 50
professionals for each 1000 pupils with an optimum load of five
teaching periods involving 125–150 pupils per day; careful coordination of subject areas throughout the school organization; adequate
facilities; provision of group activities with particular relevance for
early adolescents; and a curriculum adapted to their needs.[2]

During the past decade the percentage of school districts having
separate junior high schools rose from 40 to 53, and the total number of junior high schools increased by more than 50 per cent. This
rapid progress in attaining the form of the junior high school remains to be matched by more substantial progress in meeting the
unique purposes and needs of the junior high school student. Nevertheless, according to the National Survey of Secondary Education,
both the six-year high school and the three-year junior/three-year
senior high school typically surpass the conventional four-year high
school in quality of program.

Administrative organization of junior high schools.   There are
very few data on the national level with respect to the administrative
organization of junior high schools. One study of junior high schools
in New York State [3] revealed that there is no distinct pattern for the
performance of administrative functions at the junior high school
level among the schools studied; that administrative functions are
not being delegated to subordinates; that junior high school staffs
were inadequate numerically; that no single pattern of administrative organization and staffing is best for all junior high schools. The
study suggested the following guides for the administrative organization of junior high schools:

> An organizational flexibility which may be less important at the
> high school level, but conversely, one which requires a degree of
> adherence to basic rules and regulations which is not necessary in
> the self-contained classroom of the elementary school;
> An organization so constructed that it provides for the pupil a

---

[2] James B. Conant, *Recommendations for Education in the Junior High School
Years* (Princeton, N.J.: Educational Testing Service, 1960).

[3] Council for Administrative Leadership, *The Administrative Organization of the
Modern Junior High School* (Albany, N.Y.: The Council, 1959).

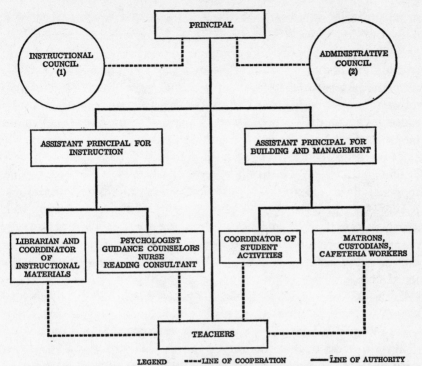

Figure 5. Organization of Ridgeway Junior High School

truly gradual transition from relative informality to a more complex and necessarily rigid operation;

Provision for the extended use of the specialist or teacher with special talent within the organizational structure;

Provision for maintaining close contact with the child as he moves from the atmosphere of the self-contained classroom;

An organization which recognizes that children will err and which creates an atmosphere in which the young adolescent will be able to test his emerging self-concept.[4]

The study suggested the following optimum staffing pattern for a junior high school of from 700–1000 pupils:

Principal, two assistant principals, school nurse, part-time or full-time psychologist, three guidance counselors, part-time or full-time

---

[4] *Ibid.,* p. 26.

coordinator of student activities, part-time or full-time coordinator of instructional materials, reading consultant, and speech correctionist.

This arrangement, for an enrollment of 850 pupils, would provide a pupil-administrator ratio of approximately 210:1 as contrasted with the actual ratio of 470:1 obtaining in the New York State junior high schools studied. One version of this organization is presented in the schematic arrangement in Figure 5.

Senior high schools.   The senior high school commonly includes Grades 9–12 or 10–12. In many smaller districts junior and senior high schools are combined in a single administrative unit of Grades 7–12. The four-year high school, although in the minority, will continue to prevail in small districts where the 8–4 plan of organization is more feasible and in states such as California, New Jersey, and Illinois, where many high schools must operate under a separate board of education and apart from elementary school districts.

With relatively few exceptions, the senior high school is a subject-centered, departmentalized, graded organization. Parallel curricula —such as general, college preparatory, commercial—are offered in all high schools except the very smallest. These curricula include some common courses but are differentiated to a considerable degree by the inclusion of specialized courses not common to the other curricula. In each curriculum some flexibility is attained through the choice of elective courses. Departures from the subject-centered curriculum are inhibited by college entrance requirements which typically specify completion of Carnegie units, subdivisions of work defined in terms of clock hours in specific subject fields. However, a number of high schools have pioneered departures from rigid curricula and departmentalization. The core curriculum is one effort in the direction of integrating substance from a number of subject fields. Class size is typically smaller in high schools than at lower grade levels.

Several interesting innovations and trends which affect school organization have been introduced in secondary schools with increasing frequency in recent years. The curriculum has been broadened and enriched. Grade placement of subject matter has been lowered. Greater academic provision has been made for individual differences for both the gifted and the slow learner. Ability-grouping and advanced placement programs have become fairly common. The school day and the school year have been lengthened in some districts. Summer schools serve both the talented and the retarded high school student. Team teaching, autoinstructional devices, television, and other electronic media have resulted in radical redeployment of pupils, faculty, time, and facilities.

One interesting departure in secondary school organization is the "school-within-a-school" organization. This concept is manifest architecturally by the campus type of school plant in which a number of small, partly self-contained units, each housing a few hundred students, exist as satellites near but apart from other small school units and the central service unit which contains the administrative offices, libraries, cafeteria, auditorium, gymnasium, and other facilities shared by all. The purpose of this concept is to combine certain advantages of small-school organization—close contact and identity among students and faculty, flexibility in scheduling and planning—with the large-school advantages of broader curriculum and more specialized services and facilities. One illustration of the administrative organization appropriate to the school-within-a-school arrangement is depicted in Figure 6. Few secondary schools are organized in this way, although more and more school systems are moving in this direction. Because this organization is greatly facilitated by the campus type of school plant, it becomes feasible only as new high school buildings are needed.

Specialized high schools. Specialized high schools are usually found in large city school districts, occasionally in smaller districts dominated by one trade or industry. Most are vocational or technical high schools, although some focus upon science, music, art, or other similar fields. Some specialized high schools are organized to serve the intellectually gifted, the physically handicapped, or the mentally retarded. However, nearly all specialized high schools require a minimum body of general education.

Comprehensive high schools. The comprehensive high school remains the predominant form of secondary education in the United States. It seeks to meet the needs of practically all youth of secondary school age with a diversified curriculum including general education; business and distributive education, among other forms of vocational education; and college preparatory education. Many very small high schools aspire to be comprehensive but are unable to meet the needs of all students because of a preoccupation with meet-

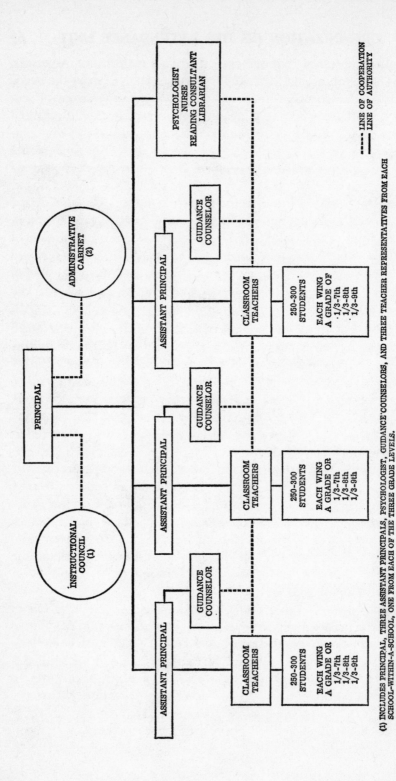

Figure 6. School-Within-A-School Organization, Junior High School

(1) INCLUDES PRINCIPAL, THREE ASSISTANT PRINCIPALS, PSYCHOLOGIST, GUIDANCE COUNSELORS, AND THREE TEACHER REPRESENTATIVES FROM EACH SCHOOL-WITHIN-A-SCHOOL, ONE FROM EACH OF THE THREE GRADE LEVELS.

(2) INCLUDES PRINCIPAL AND THREE ASSISTANT PRINCIPALS.

ing college entrance requirements. The vast majority of American youth, however, attend high schools large enough to meet the needs of most students fairly satisfactorily. Although some critics of secondary education advocate separation of academically talented students, most professional educators hope to find within the comprehensive high school the accommodations necessary to serve the needs of superior students as well as those of average and below-average students.

Administrative organization of high schools. Because of the great diversity among high schools—variations in size, function, purpose, and organization—it is difficult to define the function of secondary school administration and to describe its organization except in very general terms. Figure 7 illustrates a fairly traditional pattern of administrative organization in a large high school. The chief administrative officer of the secondary school is the principal, a line officer charged with general responsibility for the over-all operation of the secondary attendance unit. Except in very large systems, the high school principal is responsible directly to the superintendent of schools.

The functions of the secondary school principal have been defined to include:

Effective operation of the educational program
Evaluation of the educational program
Revision of the program
Selection and dismissal of personnel
Development of personnel policies
Development of good human relations
Orientation and in-service growth of personnel
Understanding of the community
Participation in community life
Involvement of the community in education
Interpretation of the school to the community
Organization of the staff
Determination of needs of funds and facilities
Operation and maintenance of materials and facilities
Establishment and maintenance of records of funds and facilities [5]

Larger high schools typically employ one or more assistant principals. The roles of assistant principal vary so widely in practice as

[5] Adapted from Cooperative Development of Public School Administration, *Your School and Staffing: Secondary School Principalship* (Albany, N.Y.: CDPSA, 1956), pp. 9–20.

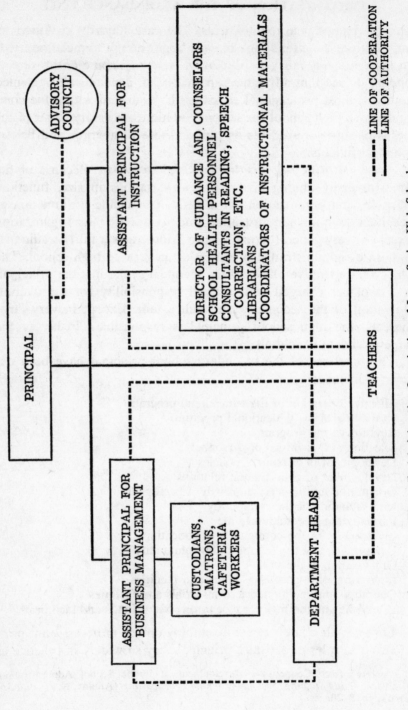

Figure 7. Administrative Organization of Large Senior High School

ADVISORY COUNCIL

PRINCIPAL

ASSISTANT PRINCIPAL FOR INSTRUCTION

DIRECTOR OF GUIDANCE AND COUNSELORS
SCHOOL HEALTH PERSONNEL
CONSULTANTS IN READING, SPEECH CORRECTION, ETC.
LIBRARIANS
COORDINATORS OF INSTRUCTIONAL MATERIALS

ASSISTANT PRINCIPAL FOR BUSINESS MANAGEMENT

CUSTODIANS, MATRONS, CAFETERIA WORKERS

DEPARTMENT HEADS

TEACHERS

- - - - - LINE OF COOPERATION
———— LINE OF AUTHORITY

to defy definition in universal terms. Figure 7 makes provision for two assistant principals whose responsibilities are well defined. One assistant principal is responsible for the business management of the high school. He attends to the fiscal affairs of the secondary unit and supervises persons responsible for the operation and maintenance of the building—custodians, matrons, and cafeteria personnel. He reports directly to the principal and relieves the principal of much of the responsibility for the management of the school's funds, facilities, and materials. The other assistant principal also reports directly to the principal, sharing with him responsibility for the leadership and coordination of the instructional program. Although the assistant principal for instruction has no line authority over teachers, he does have line authority over the specialists responsible for instructional and pupil personnel services. These personnel include the director of guidance (the "dean of students," or the "deans" respectively of boys and girls, as they are sometimes called), counselors, psychologists, nurses, and other health personnel, as well as the librarian, the coordinator of instructional materials, and consultants in reading, speech correction, and other areas.

In larger high schools faculty members are typically grouped by academic departments with someone usually designated chairman or head of the department. The department chairman is often relieved of part of his teaching load so that he may coordinate the program, materials, and facilities within a subject field. He is sometimes given line authority for the supervision of teachers, particularly new teachers, in his department. In our illustration, however, the departmental chairman's position is defined as a staff rather than line function. He cooperates in a staff relationship with teachers and the assistant principals in business and instructional functions as they relate to this department. Many schools rotate the chairmanship of the department. Some schools have abandoned department chairmen, turning their functions over entirely to instructional consultants and interdepartmental committees working on program development in conjunction with teachers and administrators.

As illustrated in Figures 4, 5, and 6, many high schools provide for various schoolwide councils. These councils advise the principal with respect to such matters as student activities or personnel policy. Sometimes they take the form of schoolwide curriculum committees which coordinate the curriculum-development function. These councils may include the principal and assistant principals, staff officers, and teachers. Teachers are often selected for membership in such councils or committees on a rotating basis.

Junior colleges.   The rapid rise of junior colleges in recent years is one of the most striking and significant developments on the educational scene. Enrollment in junior colleges has doubled in the last decade, and the number of junior colleges is expected to double during the next decade. The President's Commission on National Goals has recommended that there be a two-year college within commuting distance of most high school graduates. Presently one student in four is beginning his higher education in these institutions.

The variety of junior colleges is bewildering and their names varied: junior colleges, community colleges, extension centers, seminaries, technical institutes, and so on. These institutions serve four primary purposes: they provide terminal programs for students not going on; they provide transfer programs for students planning to complete their higher education at four-year colleges or universities; they serve as technical institutes to provide for local vocational and subprofessional needs; and they provide adult education programs. Most junior colleges offer two-year programs, although some offer one-year and others four-year programs. Approximately 15 per cent of the junior colleges are integral parts of local public school systems, and the administrative head of the junior college is responsible to the school superintendent. In some instances the superintendent of schools is also the president of the junior college. The trend is definitely in the direction of more junior colleges affiliated with the local public school system and the upward extension of public education to include two years of college work. Thus the junior college, entirely indigenous to this country, is considered a logical extension of secondary education.

Classroom Organization

School classrooms are organized vertically to handle the progression of students from the point of admission to the point of departure to the next higher school unit. Discussion of the more common patterns of classroom organization follows.

Graded organization.   The traditional vertical organization has been the graded school. The elementary school, for example, accepts five-year-olds for entry into kindergarten and, under normal circumstances, annually moves each youngster to the next successive grade until he reaches the first year of high school or junior high school where the process is continued. A specific body of subject matter is assigned to each grade level. Textbooks are designed as, say, "third-grade readers" or "fifth-grade geographies." Teachers are assigned to a particular grade level and bear such designation as "third-grade teacher." Students clearly understand which grade they are in. Promotion of the student to the next grade level is conditional upon his satisfactory completion of the requirements of his present grade. Children who fail to meet the requirements of the grade are sometimes retained in the grade for one or more years (usually not more than two).

The graded school organization has a number of apparent disadvantages. It assumes that all children should cover the same material at the same rate of speed. It forces the school to determine at the end of the year whether all or none of the material will be repeated by a youngster whose achievement is in doubt, even though his progress in part of the curriculum may have been satisfactory. Skipping grades is the usual accommodation available to the student who is capable of learning more rapidly than the norm. This adjustment is not wholly satisfactory because accelerated pupils miss contact with the material of the grades skipped. Some schools adopted plans for semiannual rather than annual promotions, but this modification reduces only in degree, not in kind, the disadvantages of the graded school and its inevitable problems of retention and promotion.

In the early twentieth century the incidence of retention was much higher than at present. Retention resulted in an increase of students over-age in grade, particularly in the upper elementary grades. Various factors led to a serious re-examination of the traditional grade organization of schools and promotion and retention policies. Research revealed that many students actually do worse when they repeat a grade than they did their first year in that grade. Nonpromotion also created for the older pupils problems of social and physical adjustment to their younger classmates, particularly in the upper grades. The incidence of school dropouts proved to be much higher among retained students. Increased understanding of children illuminated the various forces and conditions which hinder and encourage school progress. Better understanding of the phenomenon of individual differences revealed the unreality of expecting all students to progress through school at the same pace. The threat of failure proved to be an inadequate and unsatisfactory source of motivation for poorer students. Repeated retention frequently resulted in attitudes of resignation to failure with adverse social and emotional consequences. It was also recognized that retention failed to reduce appreciably the range of ability among students in a given grade. Greater homogeneity of classes did not result, and teachers were not freed of the task of providing for variability in student capabilities and achievements.

Growing concern over these consequences of retention led to an effort in most schools to adjust the graded system to the child rather than to force the child to adjust to the system. The incidence of retention was greatly reduced in most schools; many adopted the policy of automatic promotions except in unusual circumstances. Increasingly, students were placed in grades according to age and maturity rather than according to rigid specifications of academic achievement. Increased effort was made to meet the variations in student ability at all grade levels. Notwithstanding these adaptations, many educators regard the traditional graded school as an inadequate arrangement and many attempts have been made to modify or depart from graded organization.

The best-known efforts in this direction were the so-called St. Louis, Pueblo, Dalton, Cambridge, and Winnetka plans which sought to permit students to progress through the sequence of study at their own rates. Not all of those schemes were designed to break down grade lines, but all were designed to modify the effects of the graded school by helping students of differing abilities move with less of the hindrance deriving from rigid grade expectations. Although all of them have since been discontinued or greatly modified, they represented the best creative thought of their time, and were the forerunners of the present broad-scale attack on the lockstep nature of the graded school.

Multigraded and multiclass schools. The oldest prototype of the multigraded school is the one-room or two-room country school which combines students of two or more grades, sometimes as many as eight, in one classroom. As school districts enlarged through population growth have been reorganized, the number of multi-graded classrooms has been reduced sharply. However, a few school systems have re-established multigraded classrooms as a means of modifying the graded classroom. Grade designations are retained, but students may be permitted to work in several grades simultaneously according to their progress in the various subjects; for example, a child might be doing fourth-grade arithmetic, fifth-grade reading, and sixth-grade science. Other variations of this plan provide for the exchange of pupils from different grades and different classrooms for part of the school day to meet with other students of similar achievement in a given subject.

Several small high schools have developed multiclass organizations within the same room. Thus one high school classroom might include several students from one grade studying first-year French, others from other grades studying second-year French, and perhaps others studying another language, all studying under the same teacher. Autoinstructional devices such as language laboratories, teaching machines, and correspondence courses are sometimes used to facilitate such multiclass and multigrade operation. This sort of innovation is less a revolt from the strictures of graded organization than an innovation to broaden and enrich the narrow curriculum of the small high school by increasing course offerings without comparable increase in classroom sections.

Nongraded schools. "Nongraded" or "ungraded" schools may be defined as schools in which grade lines and traditional grade expectations are eliminated for a period of at least two years. Such organizations have appeared with rapidly increasing frequency over the past decade. They occur most frequently at the primary level of the elementary school, usually comprising the first three grades. The ungraded primary, for example, groups children beyond the kindergarten and below the fourth grade in classes without grade designation. Children complete the same educational experiences common to the first three grades but proceed each at his own rate with time for thorough mastery before moving on to new tasks. Most children remain in this group for three years. Some complete it in two years, others in more than three years. Sometimes the same teacher remains with the group for the entire primary unit. Students are sometimes reassigned to various subdivisions of the primary unit at intervals of several weeks to keep them with a group proceeding at a similar pace. When such reassignment prevails, it is most commonly arranged according to a series of levels in reading. Other schools group youngsters in the ungraded primary unit according to chronological age or social-emotional maturity. The nongraded school, or "continuous progress plan," as it is sometimes called, has brought corresponding changes to practices of curriculum organization, reporting pupil progress, staffing, and other aspects of school organization.

The number of school districts with ungraded primary units is estimated at 500–1000. Some schools have extended the ungraded plan through the middle grades; even a few high schools are experimenting with it. At the higher levels experimentation is more in the direction of acceleration, the more able students traveling the traditional grade route in less time. Most schools which have undertaken nongraded organization report general satisfaction with it among teachers, administrators, pupils, and parents. Much of its support derives from the logical validity of flexible groupings which permit greater accommodation of the school to the great variability in student capacity, achievement, personality, motivation, and rate of growth. It is a way of putting into practice a philosophy that values respect for the individual and recognizes the necessity for adapting the school to the child rather than the child to the school. Most of the studies so far conducted on the ungraded plan are inadequate and inconclusive comparisons of student achievement in graded and ungraded organizations. Some of the studies favor the graded organization, others the ungraded arrangement; some are indeterminate.

Dual progress plan. Another pattern of organization that has received wide attention recently is the "dual progress plan." [6] It is a semidepartmental scheme in which elementary school children are grouped according to ability for half the school day to study the "cultural imperatives"—speech, vocabulary, spelling, grammar, reading, writing, literature, and social studies. The remainder of the day is spent in an ungraded vertical system studying the "cultural electives"—mathematics, science, art, music, and foreign languages. In essence, this plan is an effort to combine the advantages

---

[6] George D. Stoddard, *The Dual Progress Plan* (New York: Harper & Row, Publishers, 1961).

of both departmentalized and self-contained classrooms and graded and ungraded organizations, with ability grouping.

Graded, multigraded, and nongraded classrooms are systems of organization which provide for the movement of students through the various levels of the educational program. The systems of organization discussed below provide for the grouping of students at the same educational level within class groups, and for their assignment to teachers.

Class size. Fundamental in any consideration of horizontal grouping is the question of how many students are to be placed in the same class. A study by the National Education Association reveals that the median size of elementary school classes in school systems in communities of over 2500 population is 30 pupils. Approximately half the elementary school classrooms in the country contain more than 30 pupils; approximately a fifth contain more than 35. There is a marked tendency for class size to increase as the population of the school district increases. Class size in the primary grades tends to be smaller than in the middle grades. According to a recent teacher opinion poll conducted by the National Education Association, the best class size for effective teaching in the elementary school is 20–25 pupils. To reduce all larger elementary school classes in the country to classes of 25 would require 92,000 new classrooms and teachers and a cash outlay of approximately $3.7 billion plus an additional $500 million for teachers' salaries and supporting services.

The median class size for all secondary schools is 27; for rural secondary schools, it is 21, and for urban secondary schools, it is 29. There appears to be great variation in the size of high school classes according to the nature of the class and the population of the community. High school classes tend to be somewhat smaller than elementary classes. Many state aid programs are based upon the assumption that secondary school classes should be smaller than elementary classes, although the rationale for this assumption has never been established in the minds of many authorities.

Many studies have been conducted to discover the optimum class size for efficient instruction. At first glance these studies appear to be inconclusive, two-fifths of them favoring small classes, one-fifth favoring large classes, and another two-fifths with no clear preference. When Blake applied fairly liberal tests of quality to these so-called research studies, he discovered that only 22 studies could pass the tests. When the results of those 22 acceptable studies were analyzed, they were found to favor smaller classes by a ratio of 5:1.[7] Thus Blake exploded a misconception still widely held; namely, that there is no research evidence to demonstrate the superiority of small classes. Subsequent studies by the Metropolitan School Study Council reinforced this finding and established other related conclusions, including the following:

> Numerical staff adequacy is a better predictor of school quality than average class size.
>
> Most of the research between 1900 and 1940 used short-term, immediately-measurable pupil achievement as a criterion. The new studies . . . have tended to use desirable classroom conditions as the criterion. They unanimously favor smaller classes, with some words of caution.
>
> Individuals are more apt to get attention in small classes.
>
> Desirable elementary classroom practices tend to be dropped when class size is increased; desirable practices are added when class size is reduced.
>
> It is patently indefensible to argue for any arbitrary, common size. Local conditions, purposes, quality desired in education, and the abilities of the teachers must be weighed.
>
> Nonclassroom personnel are at least as important as classroom teachers.[8]

The evidence in favor of smaller classes has been cited at some length here because many of the arguments for innovation in class size rest heavily on the faulty assumption that there is no evidence to support the superiority of small classes.

As indicated above, it is indefensible to argue for an arbitrary class size commonly applicable to all teaching situations. The presentation of a film or lecture and the administration of an examination are examples of functions that can be conducted far more economically and almost as well in a large group as in a small one. Discussion can probably be handled most effectively in a group of

---

[7] Howard V. Blake, *Class Size: A Summary of Selected Studies in Elementary and Secondary Schools* (New York: Ed. D. Project, Teachers College, Columbia University, 1954).

[8] Donald H. Ross and Bernard McKenna, *Class Size: The Multi-Million Dollar Question* (New York: Metropolitan School Study Council, Teachers College, Columbia University, 1955), pp. 21–22.

20–30 students. Counseling students on personal problems can usually be done most effectively with only one student at a time. Thus many schools have recently pioneered flexible groupings ranging from several hundred to ten or fewer for different educational purposes. The belief is growing that class size is best determined by the nature of the learning activity and the abilities of those teaching and being taught. This growing use of flexible groupings in both elementary and secondary programs represents a major innovation in American school organization. Carried on usually in conjunction with team teaching or educational television, these ventures are accompanied often by new patterns of staff deployment, new patterns of curriculum organization and presentation, and new patterns of utilization of space and materials.

Team teaching. The term *team teaching* is currently being applied loosely to a wide variety of collaborative teaching activity, including some arrangements that differ little from old-fashioned departmentalization, but prototypes and definitions of team teaching are legion. Ohm suggests that

> . . . a team relationship occurs when a group of teachers and students, as an organized unit, accept and carry out decision-making responsibility for a set of instructional variables such as time, space, group size, group composition, teacher assignment, and resource allocation. In addition to the variables normally under the control of the teacher, the team unit permits delegation to the instruction team of decisions usually made by the principal and the use of variables not present in the smaller, single teacher-class unit of organization.[9]

Described in operational terms, a teaching team is a group of several teachers, usually three to six, who are jointly responsible for planning, carrying out, and evaluating an educational program for a group of children. For example, a team may consist of five elementary school teachers working with 140 children in four or five typical classrooms in addition to a variety of other space including both large and small rooms. The children could all be at the same grade level, or at different grade levels. One of the teachers might be a specialist in language arts, another in social studies, another in science, another in mathematics, and another in the creative arts.

---

[9] Robert E. Ohm, "Toward a Rationale for Team Teaching," *Administrator's Notebook,* Vol. IX, No. 7 (March, 1961), 1.

Each might assume major responsibility for planning and carrying out instruction in her particular area of competence. One would be designated as team leader; all five would cooperate as an instructional team. Most team teaching projects also employ subprofessional assistants, such as teaching aides or clerical aides.

One of the best defined prototypes of team teaching at the secondary school level has been developed by the Commission on the Experimental Study of the Utilization of the Staff in the Secondary School.[10] This, a projection of "images of the future," foresees flexibility of student groupings, methods of teaching, and scheduling organized around three basic kinds of activities: large-group instruction often in groups of 100 or more, occupying about 40 per cent of the student's time; individual study or small-group study with teachers and other staff members as consultants, occupying about 40 per cent of the student's time; and discussion in small groups of 12–15 students with a teacher occupying approximately 20 per cent of the student's time. Flexibility of grouping and frequent regrouping of students are expected to cope with the differing abilities, interests, and needs of students. The proposal has interesting implications with respect to the organization of the instructional staff. It suggests a new hierarchy of faculty:

> Teacher specialists—experienced teachers with advanced professional preparation demonstrated competence, and long-term career interests and abilities
> General teachers—qualified professional personnel with less experience and perhaps only short-term career interests
> Instructional assistants—technicians selected on the basis of training and experience to do specific parts of the teaching job, such as evaluating English themes and serving as laboratory assistants
> Clerks—to perform routine duties, such as keeping records and handling supplies
> General aides—to supervise students on the school grounds, corridors, and cafeterias, and perhaps to serve as sponsors for some extracurricular activities
> Community consultants—lay members of the community used for special assignments related to their unique competencies
> Staff specialists—nonteaching professional specialists, such as guidance, research, and health service functionaries

---

[10] J. Lloyd Trump, *Images of the Future* (Washington, D.C.: National Association of Secondary School Principals, National Education Association, 1959).

Implicit in this proposed pattern of staff deployment is provision for the assignment of more highly specialized and trained professional teachers on the basis of specific rather than general duties; sharp departures in the teacher's load in the form of fewer hours per week teaching but with more time for preparation, study, and other professional tasks; release from nonprofessional duties; higher salaries for the more highly trained and more competent career teachers.

The advocates of team teaching claim that it capitalizes the unique strengths of teachers and widens the influence of good teachers; that it facilitates more efficient use of teacher time, talents, and skills; that it releases staff time for better preparation and planning; that it breaks down the isolation of the classroom and stimulates cooperation among teachers; that it promotes the in-service development of teachers; that it makes possible higher salaries and status for master teachers; and that it results in improvement of teacher morale.

Several hundred school systems are presently engaged in some form of team teaching. Whether team teaching will become an "instructional revolution," as it is being heralded by the Ford Foundation, or prove merely another educational fad, the view of some investigators, remains to be seen. If team teaching does continue to spread, it will produce a more dramatic and profound change in faculty organization and utilization than any other educational innovation ever has.

Self-contained vs. departmentalized organization.   In the self-contained classroom, the teacher-classroom is the unit of organization within the school. One teacher conducts all of the instruction for the class throughout the school day. Students typically spend the entire school day in the same room, wherein are provided all the facilities necessary for the entire program of studies. The relevance of the self-contained organizational plan to the graded school concept is evident. Each teacher can specialize in the substance of her grade level. This organizational plan is more adaptable to the core, broad-fields, and activities-centered curricula. All these curricular patterns depend upon the integration or combination of subject fields, most feasible when a single teacher is responsible for all the instruction of a class.

In a departmentalized organization the class is instructed by more than one teacher. Various teachers teach different subjects to the same class, which usually changes rooms to meet with the different teachers. "Platooning" is a pattern of partial departmentalization in which students move, but not always as the same group, from teacher to teacher for different learning activities.

The primary grade levels are most frequently organized on the self-contained basis; departmentalization is more common in the middle and upper grades. Junior and senior high schools are usually departmentalized. The core curriculum, which delegates instruction in two or more related subjects to one teacher, represents a partial movement away from the departmentalized organization in high schools.

Enthusiasm for departmentalization has shifted markedly during the present century. During the first quarter of the century departmentalization grew in frequency even though the self-contained classroom was more common at the elementary school level. By 1925 or so, debate over the virtues of departmentalization had grown intense and departmentalization was waning in elementary schools, although larger schools continued to provide special teachers for the so-called special subjects—art, music, and physical education. By 1950, departmentalization, again in favor, was becoming more frequent in elementary schools. Over the past decade the number of completely self-contained elementary classrooms was reduced by almost half, reflecting the clear trend toward partial departmentalization. However, the number of completely departmentalized elementary classrooms remained quite small—less than 4 per cent. Departmentalization seldom occurred in the lower grades, but a marked increase in the frequency of departmentalization beyond the fourth grade was evident. Large systems reported more frequent use of departmentalization. A survey of the opinions of principals indicated that they expected even greater frequency of departmentalization or partial departmentalization in the years ahead.[11]

Considerable research has been directed toward an assessment of the relative advantages of self-contained vs. departmentalized classrooms. The evidence yielded by such studies so far has been inconclusive. The chief advantage claimed for the self-contained classroom is that a teacher is able to establish better rapport and deeper understanding of children when she is in their company for

---

[11] *The Principals Look at the Schools* (Washington, D.C.: National Education Association, 1962), pp. 13, 14, 40.

a full day. It also facilitates integration of learning among the various subject fields. Departmentalization claims the advantage of permitting teachers to specialize in the instruction of a single subject or a few related subjects and, in some arrangements, for students to pass or fail individual subjects rather than entire grades. The increasing frequency of team teaching has resulted in a more widespread use of departmentalized or partially departmentalized organization.

Heterogeneous vs. homogeneous grouping. In heterogeneous classes students are grouped by age or grade, but without regard for ability or achievement. In theory, at least, homogeneous grouping brings into the same class students with similar intellectual capacity or achievement, although criteria other than intelligence and achievement are sometimes used. The terms *homogeneous grouping* and *ability grouping* are frequently used synonymously although not always properly, for students within a class may be homogeneous in point of one criterion, say achievement, but heterogeneous in ability.

Many variations of homogeneous grouping have been devised. The Detroit XYZ Plan, for example, divided children according to some criteria of achievement and learning capacity into three groups called *X, Y,* and *Z,* respectively comprising superior, average, and slow pupils. The curriculum was then differentiated for each group —the slow group receiving what might be described as minimum essentials; the superior students, a greatly enriched learning experience. Another variant of ability grouping, sometimes referred to as a "multiple track plan," divides pupils according to ability and holds the material constant for all groups but varies the periods of exposure to it according to each group's ability to master the material. Thus, average pupils might complete the elementary program in six years—bright children would require less time, slower children more. The Winnetka and Dalton plans, named after the school systems in which they were introduced, were early variants of multiple track programs.

Ability grouping, in vogue during the Twenties and Thirties, was practiced with much less frequency in succeeding years, but its popularity surged sharply in the Fifties. Many new manifestations of ability grouping have emerged in secondary schools in recent years. These include special classes for the gifted, such as honor classes and advanced placement courses. According to a recent survey,[12] the principals of half the nation's large elementary schools reported an increase in homogeneous grouping in their schools while only a few noted decreases. Nearly two-thirds of the principals at the secondary level reported an increase in homogeneous grouping. Most principals predict increased incidence of ability or achievement grouping. The most common bases reported for such grouping were judgment of teachers, scores on achievement tests, and scores on IQ tests, in that order of frequency. Ability grouping seemed to the principals to be more advantageous to the more able and the less able students than to students of average ability. This trend toward homogeneous grouping is much less apparent in small elementary and secondary schools, where there is only one section —or at most a few sections—of a particular grade and such grouping is not very feasible.

Ability grouping is defended on the grounds that it enables a school to differentiate instruction according to students' ability. It is contended that teaching and learning can be carried on more effectively when the range of ability or achievement in a given class is reduced through homogeneous grouping. Where the pace is accelerated for superior students, they are able to complete their schooling in less time and advance to higher levels sooner. The more talented students, it is claimed, are spared the boredom of a pace attuned to the abilities of slower students.

On the other hand, many studies have shown the impossibility of obtaining thoroughly homogeneous groups. When grouped by IQ, for example, students may still represent wide variation in achievement. When grouped according to achievement in, say, reading, pupils may still be widely disparate in levels of achievement in other subjects. Several studies have indicated that, regardless of the basis of homogeneous grouping used, any reduction in the range of achievement within any group is usually too small to enable a teacher to ignore the individual differences which remain. Another cogent argument against ability grouping is the effect upon the learner's self-perception as a result of his identification with a "slow" or a "fast" group. In the former case, pupils sometimes be-

---

[12] *Ibid.,* pp. 15–17.

come stigmatized by and resigned to a low esteem for their ability that may be justified only by a part of their work. Discouragement and apathy may result. Students in the "fast" group may adopt attitudes of intellectual snobbery. Teachers may be lulled into a comfortable but fallacious belief that the range of individual differences in the class has been reduced to the point where they are no longer significant and thereby defeat the very purpose of such a plan; namely, the individualization of instruction.

Considerable research has been directed toward measuring the alleged advantages of homogeneous grouping. Most of these studies have been limited to comparisons of academic achievements of students in the two types of groups. So far, the evidence fails to demonstrated conclusively the advantage of one scheme over the other. Hence the decision to group pupils in one manner or the other must be made largely on the basis of the school's educational philosophy.

An overview of the grouping dilemma. Most of the dilemmas inherent in patterns of organization, particularly horizontal organization, are not readily resolved either by empirical or experimental evidence. The variety of organizational schemes are legion, many of them of quite early origin. Much research has been directed toward their evaluation, but it has failed to demonstrate the clear-cut superiority of the self-contained over the departmentalized classroom, the homogeneous over the heterogeneous group. Part of the problem lies in the difficulty of measuring alleged advantage in terms of anything other than academic achievement which, however important, is only a part of the school's objectives. Moreover, it is difficult in experimentation to factor out significant dependent variables, such as the relationship of the pattern or organization with curriculum adaptation, instructional materials, teacher effectiveness, the "halo" effect of innovation, and others. Undoubtedly the dedication and capability of the able teacher are more essential than any grouping plan to the creation of a fine climate for learning. To put it another way: no grouping plan, however ingenious it may be, is ever a substitute for good teaching.

Elsbree and McNally have recommended several principles that are helpful in determining appropriate patterns of school organization:

1. The organization should facilitate intimate knowledge of the pupils by the teachers through extended association.

2. The organization should provide for the grouping of children in relation to the educational objectives to be sought.

3. The organization should be designed to attain greater flexibility in the use of time, space, staff, and field experiences.

4. The organization should promote unity and continuity of the learning program.

5. The organization should be in harmony with known principles of psychology, mental hygiene, and child development.

6. The organization should be simple and administratively feasible.

7. The organization should be consistent with democratic principles and processes, and should facilitate the learning and operation of them.

8. The organization should be sensibly and efficiently related to local conditions.[13]

---

[13] Willard S. Elsbree and Harold J. McNally, *Elementary School Administration and Supervision* (New York: American Book Company, 1959), pp. 135–37.

CHAPTER IV

Trends and Issues in School Organization and Staffing

In this chapter attention is given to some of the more crucial trends and issues in school organization and staffing. These are dealt with in relation to (1) the organization of the school district, (2) the organization of the administrative and supervisory staff, (3) the organization of instructional personnel, (4) the organization of students, and (5) the theories and research of organization and staffing.

Organization of School Districts

The organization and the power structure of school districts have been greatly influenced by several major forces, notably the decline of local control of education, the impact of the reorganization of school districts, and the conflict between lay and professional control of education.

Decline of local control of education. Control of education by local authorities is deeply rooted in the American heritage. As noted in Chapter 1, the control of early American schools was vested almost completely in the local community and this practice has been a time-honored tradition throughout our history. Local control of education has been regarded by many as the bulwark of our political liberty. But through the years, particularly since the Great Depression, there has been a gradual but persistent decline in local control of education. This decline has resulted from a continuous shift in the locus of power from the local educational authority to the county, state, and national levels of government. Local school districts exercise control over education within a framework of state and federal laws, regulations, and court decisions. The volume of state laws and directives regulating public education grows substantially each year, continually narrowing the latitudes of local decision-making. Through the years most states have enacted laws regulating certification, employment, payment, dismissal, and retirement of teachers; specifications for school buildings, accounting procedures, bond issues, budgets, management of school funds, and countless other aspects of school management once controlled entirely by local school authorities. The federal government has influenced education greatly through special-purpose aid directed to certain aspects of the school program—principally vocational education, mathematics, science, guidance, and languages.

Many nongovernmental agencies are also pre-empting some of the areas of decision-making which were once the sole prerogative of the local educational authority. Powerful state athletic associations exercise substantial control over interscholastic athletic activities. National testing programs, such as the College Entrance Board Examinations, have had an indirect but nevertheless powerful effect upon high school curricula. Regional agencies which accredit secondary schools have virtually forced local education authorities into making certain decisions regarding secondary education consistent with standards of accreditation set by the agencies. Other examples of control of education by nonlocal and nongovernmental agencies could be cited. The fact that such controls are nongovernmental does not make them any less real. All nonlocal agencies, both governmental and nongovernmental, limit or remove the power of school districts to make absolute decisions regarding schools and thereby circumscribe local authority over education.

The trend away from local control of education is accelerating, sometimes indirectly and subtly, sometimes obviously and forthrightly. To all appearances the trend is irreversible, however much local authorities might like it otherwise. This trend is an inevitable consequence of national and international forces and events such as the exploration of outer space; challenges to our national security; the growing complexity of our social, economic, and political structure; the mobility of our population; and many others.

Decline in local authority over education has fundamental relevance to the organization of education in the United States. Some authorities have suggested that local control of education is obsolete, that local boards of education should be disbanded and their powers turned over to state education authorities. Others regard this as heresy, and wish to reverse the trend by returning major power over education to the local community. This divergence of opinion is illustrated by the following quotations:

> Local control of the functions of education is largely responsible for the dull and uninspiring character of much school instruction. It enables local communities to protect dominant local points of view from analysis and criticism in the schools, while at the same time it deprives the teachers of any moral justification for refusing to be a party to indoctrination when it is sanctioned by a community. Teachers cannot criticize local points of view, no matter how much they may be questioned in the state or in the country.[1]
>
> Faith in the local administration of schools is a part of the democratic tradition. It is important that all the people should feel responsible for their government. In no areas is it more necessary than in the provision of public education that the thinking, desires, and ambitions of the people be made effective.[2]

The more likely probability, as the state superintendent of schools in Florida has prophesied,

> ... points to a realistic cooperative partnership of local, state, and federal governments in making possible quality education for all who can profit from such opportunities. This effort must of necessity provide for some desirable controls by all three divisions of government in the form of fiscal accounting and reporting. The initiative of local citizens to improve education at the grass roots level must not be thwarted by any effort to provide financial assistance to local schools from state and federal sources. ... The concept of local control ... is folklore and for some years has been outmoded.[3]

Impact of school district reorganization. The reorganization of school districts is having a significant impact upon school organization. Reorganized districts invariably emerge larger both in area and population—by so much, the individual citizen's opportunity to influence educational policy and program is reduced, and the board of education's capacity to interpret the educational program to the community and to energize public support is often handicapped. As several communities are combined into one school

---

[1] Myron Lieberman, *Education as a Profession* (Englewood Cliffs, N.J.: Prentice-Hall, Inc., 1956), p. 81.

[2] Educational Policies Commission, National Education Association, *The Structure and Administration of Education in American Democracy* (Washington, D.C.: The Association, 1938), p. 42.

[3] Thomas D. Bailey, "The Folklore of Local Control," *NEA Journal*, Vol. 50, No. 12 (December, 1961), 42–43.

district, local control of education is further diluted. If the communities are disparate with respect to their expectations of schools, their ability to support them, and their social values and mores, cleavages and power struggles frequently result. Very often the identity of the constituent communities is not submerged in the common interests of the new district. Representation on the board of education, even after the reorganization, may be based on the original districts rather than on the new district at large.

Conflict between lay and professional control. One of the central dilemmas in school organization grows out of controversy over what is the proper blend of lay and professional control over decisions affecting education. Disagreement arises over not only where the control should be, but also over where it actually is now. Bestor, for example, in *Educational Wastelands* contends that,

> . . . there is evidence of the debasement which the teaching profession is undergoing at the hands of the interlocking directorate of professional educationists. . . . Ceaselessly indoctrinated in official educational philosophy, subject to minute control and supervision by a professional educational hierarchy, the public school teacher cannot hope to resist administrative dictation or to secure a real voice in the formation of educational policy.

Lieberman, on the other hand, contends that the exact opposite is true:

> A sober look at the evidence indicates that . . . the professional educators are relinquishing whatever claims to professional status they might have by their acceptance—active encouragement, even—of lay determination of professional matters. [Lieberman] spurns the criticism that professional educators are seizing control of the public schools by exaggerating the scope of their professional responsibilities. While there may be individual instances of such machinations, the group as a whole is characterized by the most extreme efforts to secure lay determination of matters clearly within the scope of the educator's professional autonomy.[4]

The weight of evidence appears to be on Lieberman's side. No professional worker in our society, with the possible exception of the Protestant minister, is subject to as much lay control, practices his profession under greater public scrutiny, enjoys less professional autonomy, or is more responsive to public criticism and influence

---

[4] Lieberman, *op. cit.,* p. 106.

than the public school educator. Entry into the teaching profession, unlike entry into other professions, is regulated by certification requirements established by state boards of education which are composed largely of lay members. Courses of study and curricula, the heart of the teacher's professional autonomy, are subject to the control of a lay board of education in virtually every school system in the country. In a number of states textbooks are selected by state textbooks commissions composed largely of lay members. Add to this the number of local study groups and citizens committees that determine curriculum prescriptions, in some cases even the methods and materials by which they shall be taught, and one is forced to the conclusion that the professional prerogatives of the teacher have been endangered seriously.

The large measure of lay control of education in the United States is commonly defended on the grounds that education is a "public profession." Education is supported largely by public funds and is an enterprise of great public concern. Unless a parent is willing and able to send his child to a private school, the public school's services are inescapable. The parent has no opportunity to select the child's teacher as he would his physician, or attorney, or clergyman. Since nearly everyone is affected by the public schools, it is contended that the public should have a strong voice in determining educational policy and program through boards of education elected by the people and responsible to the people rather than to the teaching profession. These considerations are frequently invoked to defend lay control of education.

On the other hand, *public* control of education need not necessarily be *lay* control, although it has tended to be so. Boards of control over education could be composed of professional educators chosen by the public and responsible to the public. Also, boards of education could conceivably be composed of professional educators chosen by and subject to the control of practitioners, yet still exist as a public authority. However, neither of these possibilities is very probable in the context of the American educational tradition. Nevertheless, the important distinction between public control and lay control is frequently missed in discussions of the problem.

Moreover, neither public control nor lay control of education are inevitable consequences of public concern for education. The public is concerned about medical service and legal service, yet public control of medical and legal practice do not follow. The parent's interest in his child's health does not imply the parent's right to control the physician's practice. The notion that everyone should have the right to participate in every decision that interests him or affects him is exceedingly inadequate. Eligibility for participation in decision-making should be determined on the more relevant criteria of one's accountability for the consequences and his qualifications and competency for participation. If the teacher or principal or superintendent are to be responsible for the quality of education in a given classroom, their decision-making prerogatives, with respect to professional problems, should not be pre-empted. It is essential that the public not intervene between a practitioner and his conception of his professional duties and responsibilities. Hutchins has noted clearly the dangers of permitting lay decisions on professional matters:

> Academic freedom is simply a way of saying that we get the best results in education and research if we leave their management to people who know something about them. Attempts on the part of the public to regulate the methods and content of education and to determine the objects of research are encroachments on academic freedom. . . . The democratic view that the state may determine the amount of money to be spent on education and may regulate education and educators by law has nothing to do with the wholly undemocratic notion that citizens may tell educators how to conduct education and still less with the fantastic position that they may tell them how to live, vote, think, and speak.[5]

The crucial distinction here is between lay decisions on the one hand and professional decisions on the other. Generally, this distinction has not been judiciously made in American education. The traditional position on this issue has been that the board of education should have plenary power over school policies that are non-academic in nature—e.g., finance, facilities, public relations—but should act only upon the recommendations of the professional staff with respect to academic matters—e.g., content and method of teaching, selection and promotion of personnel. But in practice, laymen and even educators are often unable to make the distinction or to protect it against the powerful and sometimes subtle forces that

---

[5] Robert M. Hutchins, *The Higher Learning in America* (New Haven: Yale University Press, 1936), p. 21.

encumber it when it is made. Moreover, the separation of academic and nonacademic affairs is often difficult because the two are often contingent.

Given the strong tradition of lay control over education in this country and a teaching force that tolerates—indeed, even encourages—a high degree of lay encroachment upon its professional prerogatives, no great redress is likely. The public must defend its right to decide on matters which are essentially nonprofessional in nature, but it must entertain the professional advice available. Likewise, educators must insist upon autonomy over matters that are primarily professional in nature, but entertain advice from outside the profession. This will continue to be a difficult effort, one that will be often misunderstood. George Bernard Shaw once defined a profession as "a conspiracy against the laity." Others have argued that when an occupation becomes self-conscious of its professional prerogatives, it inevitably lays claim to powers of self-regulation which hint of monopolistic privilege. One is reminded of William Pitt's admonition that "unlimited power is apt to corrupt the minds of those who possess it." But power and autonomy are not inherently corrupt unless they are sought only to succor professional vanity or for selfish trade union purposes. The essential reason for professional authority must be to improve the competence of the teaching force and thereby to improve its service to youth and society. No other purpose is justified. No other purpose is worthy of a profession. To take a cue from Lord Macaulay, "the highest proof of virtue is to possess boundless power without abusing it."

Organization of the Administrative and Supervisory Staff

Several basic issues and trends with respect to the organization of the administrative and supervisory staff will now be examined: the impact of larger school districts on the administrative structure; the charge of overadministration of the educational enterprise; the conflict of sources of authority; the conflict in role expectations in school administration; and the issues regarding the structure of the administrative and supervisory staff.

Impact of larger school districts. School districts are growing rapidly in enrollment as a result of reorganization, population growth, and increased holding power. Because these larger districts require larger staffs and larger administrative organizations, the number of chief local school administrators has sharply declined while the number and variety of administrative specializations has greatly expanded. The demand for school business managers, curriculum coordinators, and directors of curriculum, research, adult education, personnel, public relations, and other administrative functions continues to increase. These new specialists tend to see only a segment of the total administrative operation. Administration tends to become fractionated. The chief administrator is confronted with the task of helping to fit together the efforts of the larger staff.

Larger administrative units, despite their other advantages, complicate the administrative processes. Planning, coordination, communication, evaluation, reporting, and decision-making all become more complex. Interpersonal relations grow as geometric progressions. Lines of authority grow longer and sometimes more obscure. More levels are added to the administrative hierarchy and the distance between the teacher and the chief school administrator is increased. Forced to relinquish many of the controls over instruction to individual schools, the central office becomes more and more preoccupied with systematic responsibilities in the realm of business management. Committees, councils, and other forms of small group action are built into the structure, either formally or informally, to accomplish those tasks once handled by the entire faculty, now grown too large to constitute an effective work group. The once easygoing, face-to-face contacts of subordinates and superiors gives way to more bureaucratic and impersonal relations. More and more deliberate attention must be given to the problem of keeping the organizational structure itself working smoothly, a much simpler problem in small districts. The twentieth century phenomenon of bigness which has overtaken government, corporations, labor unions, and many other enterprises is now rapidly overtaking our schools with all its consequences, good and bad.

The charge of overadministration. Some critics of the educational scene have viewed with alarm the growth of the administrative hierarchy and its impact upon the educational enterprise. Vice-Admiral Rickover testified before a Congressional committee that one of the most urgent reforms needed in American education is the elimination of all nonteaching principals and superintendents, a preposterous proposal without precedent in any other field of human enterprise. Goodman, in *The Community of Scholars,* identifies the chief enemy of American education as topheavy administration, "a cancerous growth" which has become overly responsive to irrelevant public pressures. He states that there are more school administrators in New York State alone than in all of Western Europe— the ratio of public school administrators to faculty in America is 30:100; in Israel, 3:100. But a study of public school administrative organization in New York State revealed the inaccuracy of Goodman's data—only nine administrators for every 100 faculty; many administrative staffs were still critically inadequate numerically; and increases of 25 to 160 per cent seemed in order.[6]

The question of the numerical adequacy of administrative staffs cannot be answered categorically. Adequacy is relative to the dimensions of the task. As long as the people of this country insist that schools serve hot lunches, collect money for charities, field fancy bands with half a hundred baton twirlers and cheerleaders, stage athletic extravaganzas, dispatch transcripts and recommendations for each senior to a half-dozen colleges, handle governmental red tape, and conduct essay contests ad infinitum, little reduction in administrative personnel is possible. Society has transferred more and more responsibilities to the school. The public school has become all things to all people, responsible not only for the intellectual development of the child but also for his physical, moral, social, emotional, and vocational development. Whether or not all these activities are defensible educationally is another matter. The point is that it is irresponsible to insist upon a reduction in the administrative staff without tackling the prior question of which administrative functions can be abandoned and proving that administrators' work loads are too light. Neither of these problems is likely to yield to facile solutions.

The charge of overadministration poses another dilemma: the choice between "tight" and "loose" organization. The tightly organized school system is distinguished by such characteristics as well-defined lines of authority and responsibility, clear-cut statements of policies and regulations, written job descriptions, impersonality in

---

[6] Cooperative Development of Public School Administration, *Your Schools and Staffing: Current Practice in Administrative Staffing in New York State* (Albany, N.Y.: CDPSA, 1955), p. 10.

the interactions of its members, and close supervision and control of subordinates by superiors. The tight organization is rationalized by invoking the importance of improving teacher performance, of exercising quality control, of insuring efficiency, and of achieving coordination and maximization of effort, among other prudential considerations. Overadministration, it is alleged, is responsible for much of teachers' dissatisfaction, the rise of the "organization man" lacking in individuality and imagination, and the sterility of educational practice.

The loosely organized school system is distinguished by such characteristics as the absence of well-defined lines of authority and responsibility, lucid policy statements and job descriptions; heavy dependence upon personal relations rather than bureaucratic structure; high autonomy of individual schools and teachers; and loose supervision in a generally permissive work climate. The loose organization is rationalized by such considerations as the importance of encouraging creativity and adaptation, of stimulating teacher morale through increased freedom, of protecting the teacher's professional autonomy, and of avoiding the deleterious effects of regimentation and orthodoxy. The loose organization is criticized on the grounds that responsibility and accountability are diffused, quality control is lost because of the absence of norms, integrity of program is weakened by the absence of standardized practices and procedures, and that a *laissez-faire* atmosphere results.

Moeller's study, which is particularly relevant to this dilemma, concluded that the bureaucracy, an orderly, understandable, and predictable form of organization, does not induce in teachers a feeling of powerlessness or alienaton from the system; but that it offers teachers more opportunity to influence the direction of the enterprise, assures them of specific avenues of communication up the line to the decision-making centers of administration, guarantees them the best possible working conditions within the limits of available resources, and presses toward effectiveness of operation and efficiency in employment of personnel.[7]

Certainly the professional autonomy of teachers in some school systems has been severely circumscribed through classroom inspections by administrators and supervisors made in the name of "super-

---

[7] Gerald H. Moeller, "Bureaucracy and Teachers' Sense of Power," *Administrator's Notebook*, Vol. 11, No. 3 (November, 1962), 3–4.

vision." Assumptions have been made about "best" methods of teaching and the reliability of observers' judgments of teaching performance that are not supported by research data. Moreover, the deleterious effect of close supervision upon morale of most teachers is well known. In too many cases excessively rigorous supervision and control have coerced teachers into orthodox and stereotyped teaching methods and discouraged creativity, imagination, and experimentation. In other professions, after a practitioner's competency has been established through a period of carefully supervised probationary service, the professional is presumed to be competent and relieved of close supervision to a degree far beyond that presently granted the public school teacher in many systems.

An enlightened and realistic point of view with respect to character and intensity of administrative control and supervision is emerging in many schools. This concept is based upon a permissive, nondirective strategy that offers wide latitudes for teacher individuality within minimal limits of prudential control. The autonomy of both the teacher and the individual school is respected and strengthened. Administration and supervision are viewed as supportive, stimulating, and suggestive, rather than as commanding, coercive, and controlling. The administrative structure which supports this philosophy of administration is illustrated by the case description of the Ridgeway organization in Chapter 2.[8]

Conflict of sources of authority. A classic concept in organizational theory is the principle of unity of command; i.e., a person can be accountable to only one superior. To put it more simply: a person should have only one boss. Let us examine this principle with respect to the superintendent of schools.

In all organizational charts there is a neat single line drawn vertically from the superintendent of schools upward to the board of education. Another single line extends upward from the board of education to the community. Below the superintendent is a single line drawn to the principal and on to the teacher. It looks simple and pure. In reality it is far less simple. People won't stay in their boxes or follow the lines drawn on the chart. Moreover, the boxes

---

[8] For an extended treatment of an enlightened and humane point of view regarding administrator-staff relations, see William B. Castetter, *Administering the School Personnel Program* (New York: The Macmillan Company, 1962), Chap. 3.

contain all kinds of people with quite disparate values and expectations.

The most critical and central need in American education is for a precise and acceptable statement of the task of education: What is the purpose of education? Until this question is answered with some clarity, any school organization is likely to founder and suffer public criticism. Organizational structure is derived from the purpose which the organization seeks to attain. When the purpose is poorly defined or in dispute, so must be the organization also. Unfortunately, the definition of the school's task has always been the subject of wide disagreement. The local boosters' association may attach major importance to fielding a winning football team while the association of university women regards interscholastic athletics as an expendable frill. The local ministerial association may regard the development of moral and spiritual values as the central task of the school and insist upon Bible reading and prayer while the American Civil Liberties Union regards this as an unwarranted invasion of private religious beliefs. The League of Women Voters may encourage the school to devote more attention to teaching about the United Nations while a veterans' organization tries to forbid it.

The administrative organization, particularly the superintendent, is invariably caught at the intersection of these conflicts with multiple lines of accountability and a whole field of forces and sanctions impinging upon him, a neat organizational chart notwithstanding.[9]

Let us examine this chaos in more detail. First, the superintendent of schools is responsible to a number of governmental agencies beyond the board of education. State laws, regulations of the state board of education and state department of education, rulings of the attorney general, state and federal court decisions—all impose certain mandates and sanctions directly upon the superintendent of schools. Various other state agencies, such as the departments of health, labor, and public safety, in addition to various federal agencies, such as the Veterans Administration and the Department of Agriculture, also impose certain obligations upon the superintend-

---

[9] For an extended discussion of the conflict of outside forces and their efforts to control school administration, see Neal Gross, *Who Runs Our Schools?* (New York: John Wiley & Sons, Inc., 1958), Chaps. 1–6.

ent. Some of these mandates exist apart from or even in conflict with the mandates of the board of education. These obligations emanating from governmental agencies—local, county, state, and national—constitute the legal source of authority and responsibility under which school administration operates.

Within the local, state, and national communities many extralegal organizations and forces exercise authority over the superintendent of schools. College admission authorities, regional accrediting associations, national testing programs, state athletic associations, alumni associations, veterans' groups, civic associations, parents' groups, business organizations, churches, and political parties often press their extralegal but nevertheless real and powerful influences upon the superintendent. They are often successful in exercising very real authority over the superintendent's decisions and actions. As one city superintendent of schools put it,

> I am really not an educator, I'm a politician and a public relations functionary. I spend my time struggling with race problems, raising funds, negotiating with labor unions, arguing with tax equalization boards, pacifying parent groups, begging the support of the chamber of commerce for our next bond issue, needling tax collectors, intervening in juvenile court in behalf of wayward kids, soliciting the help of social workers, helping the police run down vandalism on school grounds, and appeasing newspaper editors.

A third family of forces which claims authority over school administration is the profession itself. Unfair or unethical administrative action can elicit reprisals and sanctions upon the school district from powerful teachers' associations or unions. Codes of professional ethics established by the profession impose limits upon the administrator's decision-making authority. The power generated by the local teachers' association is sometimes formidable, as illustrated in the case of the Ridgeway schools in Chapter 2. The opinion or will of the school faculty is a very real authority that the superintendent can ignore only at great peril. The success image of the school administrator's own professional reference group may have powerful influence upon his behavior.

Finally, the superintendent's authority derives in part from his own professional knowledge and competence. Depending upon the tolerances of his own conscience, he can compromise his own pro-

fessional judgment and values only to the extent that he is able to
live with himself and maintain his self-respect.[10]

Governmental, community, professional, and personal sources of
authority interact and converge, very often in contradiction of each
other, to shape the behavior of the school administrator. They are
sometimes vague, inarticulate, and changeable; sometimes strident,
unyielding, and intolerant. But they all have their impact upon the
organization of the school. Organization, as we have seen, is an
effort to clarify and distribute responsibility and authority among
individuals and groups in an orderly manner consistent with the
purposes of the enterprise. Obviously, when the purposes of the
enterprise are confused, the test of consistency with purpose cannot
be applied to the organizational structure. When the faculty, board
of education, superintendent, public and subpublics, and state and
federal agencies are in dispute regarding educational purpose, program, and policy, responsibility and authority cannot be agreed
upon and discharged effectively. The disputing parties climb all
over the organizational chart, ignoring established lines of authority, creating their own lines—formally if possible, informally if
necessary—grasping for power in any way they can. Organization
becomes confused and disorderly. Citizens' committees may be
formed to help resolve the controversy, and the superintendent may
suddenly discover that he has a new line of authority to the community that runs through the citizens' committee rather than through
the board of education. He is now working for two bosses, and the
principle of unity of command is compromised. To keep peace with
the faculty, the superintendent may draw another circle on his organizational chart and label it "teachers' advisory council." The
school principal then realizes that the teachers on this council now
have direct access to the boss, and exercise some authority over the
principal who is thus also working for two bosses. So it goes. Until
the sources of authority over school administration are clarified, if
indeed they ever can be, organization will remain confused and disorderly, at least to some degree.

Conflict in role expectations.   Related to the conflict in sources
of authority is the conflict of role expectations with respect to the

---

[10] For further discussion of sources of authority, see H. Thomas James, "The
Nature of Professional Authority," *Phi Delta Kappan,* Vol. XL, No. 2 (November, 1959), 45–48.

school administrator and the administrative organization. An illustration of this conflict is implicit in the ubiquitous definition of the superintendent's role as "executive officer of the board of education and professional leader of the school faculty." The incompatibility of these roles is frequently evident. For example, as the executive officer of the board, the superintendent of schools will be required at times to recommend that salary increments be denied teachers whose work is not satisfactory. But such recommendation may seriously jeopardize his acceptability as the professional leader of those teachers. Teachers generally may see the school administrator primarily as a campaigner for better salaries and fringe benefits, protector of teachers from merit salary programs, defender of teachers and schools against attack, and provider of funds and facilities. Board members may see the superintendent as an economizer of school funds, a faculty disciplinarian, a hardnosed executor of school board policy, and a courageous and just evaluator of the educational enterprise. Parents may expect the superintendent to be a defender of student welfare, a campaigner for better educational opportunity for children and youth, an effective leader of the annual Red Cross drive, and an entertaining and fluent public speaker available to community groups six nights a week. The ultimate conflict between these sometimes irreconcilable expectations is further confounded by confusion of the administrator's sources of authority, noted earlier. Enterprising school administrators seek to reconcile these role conflicts as much as possible through clarification of responsibilities, by cooperative study of administrative organization, and by development of job descriptions. School administrators with vision and courage are often able to reduce the conflict in demands made upon them.

Many issues and conflicts arise with respect to the nature of the administrative organization itself. A discussion of the more important issues of administrative organization follows.

Horizontal vs. vertical organization. The horizontal organization vs. the vertical organization dilemma raises the question of whether central administrative and supervisory personnel should be assigned responsibility along grade levels in school organization (horizontal organization) or along some function or subject field irrespective of grade levels (vertical organization). The elementary school supervisor and the director of adult education are examples of positions in a horizontal organization. The business manager and the director of music are examples of positions in a vertical organization. The horizontal organization implies that it is the grade levels of the school organization upon which division of responsibility is logically to be based. The vertical organization implies that specialization and division of responsibility derive more logically from subject areas, such as music and physical education, or from homogeneous functions, such as guidance and business management, that cut across grade lines. The horizontal organization tends to coordinate effort, policy, and practice along the same or neighboring grade lines across various subject fields and functions; the vertical organization tends to coordinate individual subject fields or functions throughout the school system irrespective of grade lines.

A major difficulty arises when a school system combines vertical and horizontal organization indiscriminately. This often results in overlapping responsibilities and gaps in responsibilities. For example, the director of music (vertical organization) and the director of elementary education (horizontal organization) would both presumably have responsibility for music instruction in the elementary schools. Regardless of the system or combination of systems used, clarity of responsibility and its orderly distribution are fundamental imperatives.

Line and staff vs. "purpose" organization. The issue is whether there is an alternative to the line and staff concept. A line officer—the principal, for example—is one who holds power and authority over subordinates. A staff officer—the director of research, for example—is one who holds no authority over subordinates (except for his own office staff) and whose function is service or advisement rather than control. The line and staff concept, then, refers to a system of administrative organization that recognizes the need for lines of authority and accountability and which accordingly distinguishes between line and staff officers in an organization. It has been attacked by some writers as being rigid, arbitrary, undemocratic, and needlessly complex. Some of its critics have proposed instead a "purpose based" type of organization that attempts to set the purposes of the institution into relationship with each other.[11] Unfortunately, all such attempts omit people and positions, neglect to

---

[11] See, for example, Alfred H. Skogsberg, "Basing Staff Organization on Purpose," *Phi Delta Kappan*, Vol. 36, No. 6 (March, 1955), 213–19.

illuminate the inevitable power relationships, and fail to provide for an orderly distribution of authority and responsibility.

The only alternative to orderly distribution of authority through well-defined lines of accountability appears to be chaos. The exercise of authority is essential and inescapable in any enterprise. Authority may be exercised wisely or unwisely, democratically or arbitrarily, but the line and staff concept per se does not ordain the manner of its exercise. There is nothing inherently democratic or undemocratic about the line and staff concept; it is only in the application that it becomes one or the other. For the present at least, there appears to be no meaningful alternative to the distribution of authority through some sort of line and staff construction, although there is of course unlimited variety in the manner of its construction.

Tall vs. flat organization. This issue poses the question of how many levels of authority ought to exist in the administrative hierarchy between the chief administrative officer and the rank and file. The tall organization is characterized by many; the flat, by few. The tall organization provides for a great number of line officers, but each has a narrow sphere of responsibility. Specialists tend to become line rather than staff officers. Individual schools have reduced autonomy. The flat organization, on the other hand, employs fewer line officers; they have broad responsibilities and operate fundamentally as generalists. Specialists operate as service arms of the classroom and tend to become staff rather than line officers. Individual schools have greater autonomy and the building principal assumes major responsibility for the total educational program of the students in his school.

Decentralized vs. centralized organization. This issue is related to the flat vs. tall dilemma. A tall organization, although not inherently centralized, tends by its nature to centralize authority at the top, whereas the flat organization tends to decentralize authority, although not invariably so. The advantages of decentralization include the making of decisions by people closer to the affected point and its context, and by the people who must make the decisions work. The disadvantages of decentralization include the natural reluctance of some executives to delegate authority and the increased possibility of lack of uniformity of decisions within the organization.

Span of control issue.   This issue is also somewhat related to the tall vs. flat dilemma. A classic principle of organization, now the center of some dispute, is the belief that an administrator can supervise directly the work of no more than six subordinates and should have no more than that number reporting directly to him. This concept is based upon the assumption that the executive's span of attention cannot accommodate a larger sphere, and that more than six subordinates hopelessly complicate the relationships. Many authorities now believe that it is possible for an administrator to supervise the work of a larger number of executives, particularly if the supervision need not be too close or too direct, and if the work of the subordinates is not highly interrelated.

A strict application of the limited span of control principle reduces the number of subordinates that can exist at any level of authority and thereby increases the number of levels of authority needed, an inclination to a taller organization structure. Thus, the issues of centralization vs. decentralization, tall vs. flat structure, and the span of control principle tend to be related in practice. There is no easy solution to these dilemmas. The answers require value judgments. With respect to schools, the issues focus on such operational questions as: Is more systemwide uniformity of practice to be desired at the expense of the adaptability of local schools to neighborhood needs? Is closer supervision and control of subordinates' work to be desired at the expense of individual creativity and initiative? Is greater uniformity of decisions to be desired at the expense of decisions made closer to the point of action by the persons who will be committed to implement them? Is it more desirable for specialists to operate as line officers or as staff officers? Obviously there are no categorical answers to these questions. It is, however, essential that they be faced deliberately and that thoughtful attention be given to their consequences in developing an administrative structure.

Unit vs. multiple control issue.   This issue raises the question of whether an organization can operate effectively with more than one chief executive. The principle of unit control—or "unity of command," as it is sometimes called—is well established in the theory of administrative organization. No other concept is compatible with the criterion of orderly distribution of authority and responsibility. No one can work as effectively for two or more bosses as he can for one. Nevertheless, multiple control is fairly common in school organization. One manifestation results from the practice of having a school business manager coordinate with the superintendent of schools and report directly to the board of education. In this circumstance the school system has two bosses. Actually, the business dimension and the educational dimension of school administration cannot be separated without imperiling the school system's organizational wellbeing. The decision of whether the purchase of pianos or kilns must be eliminated to reduce the school budget has both financial and educational implications of interest to both the business manager and the superintendent. To whom will the board of education turn in such matters? Trouble arises when the organizational structure places them both in coordinate positions.

Another violation of the unity of command principle arises frequently between the supervisor and the principal, particularly when both function as line officers. The teacher is often caught between conflicting sets of expectations or commands from two bosses. The reading supervisor may, for example, require one form of behavior in the second-grade teacher while the principal requires another, and both are only exercising their duly constituted authorities. This problem does not result when the specialist is placed in a staff position. In this case, the reading supervisor becomes a reading consultant or helping teacher and is regarded as a member of the principal's staff while in his school. In case of conflict, the teacher now clearly perceives the principal as her only immediately superior line officer. The resolution of the issue of unit vs. multiple control can be stated categorically: multiple control is unjustifiable organizationally, wherever it occurs.

Institutional vs. individual dilemma. This issue arises frequently from conflict between the purposes, values, and expectations of the individual and the purposes, values, and expectations which the institution places upon his position. In a perfect state of affairs, the personal and the institutional expectations and values would be congruent. But such is not often the case. The institutional concept centers attention upon job descriptions which define the work assignments of positions in terms of institutional purposes closely related to the total organizational plan. It derives strength from its contribution to the logical, orderly, systematic distribution of authority and responsibility within the organization. The specifications for work assignment are independent of an incumbent although his personal characteristics will certainly influence to some degree the character of the position while he holds it. The institutional concept facilitates orderly decision-making by clarifying lines of responsibility and areas of jurisdiction.

A job description is an analysis of the functions, responsibilities, and authority which reside in a particular position and the relationship of that position to others in the organization. Although job descriptions have not been widely used in educational organizations, their evident success in other enterprises suggests that many values might accrue from their use in schools. The job description makes explicit the administrator's role and function in the organization, his latitudes of authority and responsibility, and his relationship vis-à-vis others in the organization. The job description adds to the personal security of the employee, reduces the possibility of overlapping responsibilities and gaps between responsibilities, and furthers teamwork and coordination of effort.[12]

The individual or "personal" concept, as it is sometimes called, suggests that job descriptions are not only unnecessary but undesirable. It argues that such efforts are not appropriate for positions in a complex and dynamic social institution where the artistic dimension of the job is at least as large as the scientific dimension. It insists that efforts to prescribe limits of action and responsibility tend to deaden initiative and creativity. It suggests that the institution should instead hire broadly qualified people and let them work out their own work assignments to accommodate their own interests and expectations as well as possible with those of the institution. Insofar as it fails to make the individual's role explicit and encourages constant change in role as positions are filled by different people, it leads to disruption and inefficiency. The solution to this dilemma cannot be stated categorically. The best choice in most cases would appear to lie somewhere between the extremes. In the interests of distributing authority and responsibility in an orderly manner, the institution can hardly evade the necessity of establishing job de-

---

12 For model job descriptions of the superintendent, principal, staff specialists, and school business manager, see Daniel E. Griffiths, *et al., Organizing Schools for Effective Education* (Danville, Ill.: The Interstate Printers and Publishers, 1962), Chaps. 10–13.

scriptions. However, these descriptions should be sufficiently general in most instances to permit incumbents to exercise a fair measure of initiative and imagination.

Organization of Instructional Personnel

The new patterns of staff utilization emerging from team teaching and the use of the mass media and autoinstructional devices promises one of the most radical changes in school organization. These innovations, if continued, will change dramatically the conventional organization and deployment of teachers, administrators, and instructional specialists. Present patterns of team teaching reject the constant grouping of 20–30 students with one teacher, and even depart drastically from former patterns of departmentalization. Team teaching places several members of a teaching team in joint responsibility for a large number of students who are arranged in groups of various sizes at different times for different kinds of activity. The autonomy of the individual teacher and his class is abandoned in team teaching. Responsibility for instruction is shared, and the determination of accountability for educational progress is complicated. In team teaching the coordinate status of all teachers within the organization is destroyed by the designation of some teachers as "team leaders" or "master teachers." Moreover, the power relationship between the principal and his faculty is disturbed as team leaders assume some responsibilities for the direction of other teachers' work.

So far there is insufficient evidence on the crucial question of whether the subdivision of the teaching function into specialized parts undertaken by individual members of the teaching team is a more productive use of teacher time and talent than the traditional unity of the teaching function in the single teacher-classroom situation. Some authorities ask whether the specialization of teaching functions may split the central unity of teaching and fractionate authority and accountability. As one authority put it; . . . in many so-called "team" enterprises, what actually exists is merely a voluntary federation of sovereign teachers enjoying a cooperative collaborative relationship, but within which no one can be held specifically accountable for failures of communication, of program integration, or of performance.[13] There is also the question of whether the effort required to control and coordinate the variables introduced by team teaching is worth whatever effect these variables have upon teaching efficiency. Certainly team teaching has a significant impact upon the basic organizational structure of the school, affecting authority, power structure, status, teacher-principal relationships, and the whole system of motivation and rewards. Whether or not this impact is advantageous or deleterious is not yet clearly evident from research evidence. One authority warns that team teaching, with its focus upon the form rather than the substance of teaching, its preoccupation with organization, its moving about of children, teachers, and subjects, may divert us from facing up to the hard task of improving teaching in its broadest sense.[14]

The introduction of educational television also alters school organization. The most able teachers are usually selected for televised presentations. Salary and status increments for these teachers are likely to follow. The power of these teachers to control the substance and method of instruction is greatly extended. The introduction of programmed and television instruction have also introduced a number of new positions in the educational organization, such as educational programmers and various technical specialists.

Another innovation in staff utilization is the introduction of teacher aides and other subprofessional or paraprofessional personnel, often in conjunction with team teaching but sometimes as a hedge against increases in class size. The use of these subprofessional personnel reportedly results in more efficient use of professional time and facilitates experimentation with staffing.

In summarizing the impact of new patterns of staff utilization, Wynn and DeRemer reached the following conclusions:

> Although most experiments did not result in any over-all saving of professional time or money (as was once predicted and sought), a substantial amount of time was reallotted among tasks. There is little doubt that the role of the teacher would change significantly

[13] Robert H. Anderson, "Team Teaching," *NEA Journal,* Vol. 50, No. 3 (March, 1961), 52.

[14] Anne Hoppock, "Team Teaching: Form without Substance?" *NEA Journal,* Vol. 50, No. 4 (April, 1961), 48.

if the new technology were widely used. . . . Perhaps the most fateful possibility inherent in the new technology was that the television director, the motion picture editor, and the teaching machine manufacturer might preempt the curriculum building function of the teacher more than the textbook author ever did.[15]

Organization of Students

The major trends with respect to the organization of pupils for instruction have been presented in Chapter 3. They include (1) greater flexibility with respect to class size, and greater movement of students among groups; (2) increased departure from the self-contained classroom, particularly in the middle and upper grades, but toward forms of partial rather than complete departmentalization; (3) increased use of homogeneous grouping; (4) increased frequency of nongraded organization, particularly in the primary grades; (5) trend from the 8–4 organization toward the 6–6 and 6–3–3 patterns; and (6) the increased incidence of special classes and special schools for the mentally retarded and the educationally advanced students.

In general, research has failed to establish clearly the superiority of one pattern of grouping over others. For answers to the grouping problems, schools must, for the present at least, turn to their own educational philosophies for guidance. If the school is dedicated to the concept of a curriculum of pre-established essentials, organized around subject matter content, set in sequence, requiring mastery by arbitrary standards of achievement by all students, then the graded, departmentalized school with some form of homogeneous grouping follows. If the school holds an organismal view of human development with emphasis upon social, emotional, and physical development as well as mental development, and believes that education should be life-centered, that knowledge among the subject fields should be integrated and related, then an ungraded, heterogeneous, largely self-contained scheme of grouping would seem to be more appropriate.

---

[15] D. Richard Wynn and Richard W. DeRemer, "Staff Utilization, Development, and Evaluation," *Review of Educational Research,* Vol. 31, No. 4 (October, 1961), 396.

Theory and Research on
Organization and Staffing

The organization of school districts, boards of education, and attendance units has been widely researched through the years. Knowledge of these aspects of school organization is fairly adequate although conclusive answers to many issues remain to be found. The *Encyclopedia of Educational Research* and the *Review of Educational Research* provide quite useful summaries of the major relevant research projects.

A major aspect of organization which escaped the illumination of research until quite recently is the internal organization of the school system both as an administrative process and as a social system. Fortunately the volume of theoretical formulations and research has begun to grow. More attention is being given to the socio-psychological dimension of the dynamics of human activity than to the mechanics of organization. Griffiths' model of administration as decision-making has become a useful concept for the study of administration generally and organization particularly.[16] This kind of model reveals the organization in motion, illuminates its power structure, and offers some operational measures of organizational performance. Getzels' model of administration as a social process and school organization as a social system is most useful in clarifying the dichotomy of institutional vs. individual goals and conflicts, facilitating the study of the interaction of these forces.[17] Argyris has directed systematic attention to the relationship between organization and personality.[18] A practical guide for the study of administrative staff organization and case studies of administrative organization in school systems of various sizes has appeared.[19]

More and more school systems are giving deliberate and scholarly thought to the evaluation and reconstruction of their administrative organization. This new ferment in the study of organization as an administrative process is sorely needed and long overdue as

---

[16] Daniel E. Griffiths, "Administration as Decision Making," in Andrew W. Halpin, ed., *Administrative Theory in Education* (Chicago: Midwest Administration Center, University of Chicago, 1958), pp. 119–49.

[17] Jacob W. Getzels, "Administration as Social Process," *op. cit.*, pp. 150–65.

[18] Chris Argyris, *Personality and Organization* (New York: Harper & Row, Publishers, 1957).

[19] Griffiths, *et al., op. cit.*, Chaps. 4–9, 16.

school organization struggles to keep pace with the heavy burdens of sharply rising enrollments, expanded staff, increased services to youth and society, and growing complexity of the school's relationship to society. This new knowledge casts grave doubt on Alexander Pope's classic admonition: "For forms of government let fools contest; whate'er is best administer'd is best." Clearly school organization cannot be best administered unless the organization itself is a rational plan for the efficient deployment of manpower in harmony with the purposes of the institution and consistent with the best theory on organization.

Bibliography

American Association of School Administrators, *School District Organization*. Washington, D.C.: The Association, 1958. 323 pp.

————, *Educational Administration in a Changing Community*. Washington, D.C.: The Association, 1959. 221 pp.

Cooper, Shirley, Howard A. Dawson, and Robert M. Isenberg, "School District Organization," *Encyclopedia of Educational Research*. New York: The Macmillan Company, 1960. Pp. 1194–1203.

Council for Administrative Leadership, *The Administrative Organization of the Modern Junior High School*. Albany, N.Y.: The Council, 1959. 48 pp.

Davies, Daniel R. and Laurence Iannaccone, "Ferment in the Study of Organization," *Teachers College Record*, Vol. 60, No. 2 (November, 1958), 61–72.

Dean, Stuart E., *Elementary School Administration and Organization*, Bulletin 1960, No. 11. Washington, D.C.: U.S. Office of Education, 1960. 126 pp.

"Elementary School Organization, Purpose, Patterns, Perspective," *The National Elementary Principal*, Vol. 41, No. 3 (December, 1961), 1–157.

Griffiths, Daniel E., David L. Clark, D. Richard Wynn, and Laurence Iannaccone, *Organizing Schools for Effective Education*. Danville, Ill.: The Interstate Printers and Publishers, 1962. 338 pp.

Keller, Robert J., "Secondary Education—Organization and Administration," *Encyclopedia of Educational Research*. New York: The Macmillan Company, 1960. Pp. 1241–59.

Kreitlow, Burton W., "Organizational Patterns: Local School Districts," *Review of Educational Research*, Vol. 31, No. 4 (October, 1961), 380–92.

Philadelphia Area School Study Council, *Staffing Schools for Essential Services*. Philadelphia: The Council, Temple University, 1957. 20 pp.

Reeves, Charles E., *School Boards: Their Status, Functions, and Activities*. Englewood Cliffs, N.J.: Prentice-Hall, Inc., 1954. 368 pp.

Shane, Harold G. and James Z. Polychrones, "Elementary Education Organization and Administration," *Encyclopedia of Educational Research*. New York: The Macmillan Company, 1960. Pp. 421–30.

Trump, J. Lloyd, *Images of the Future*. Washington, D.C.: National Education Association, 1959. 46 pp.

Index

Index

A

Ability grouping, 77-79
Adequacy of staff, 34-36, 59-60, 72, 88-89
Administration:
  adequacy of, 34-36, 72, 88-89
  adult education, 35
  educational program, 41-42
  elementary schools, 52-56
  health services, 36
  historical development, 18-19, 28-31
  issue of overadministration, 88-91
  professionalization of, 29
  role conflicts in, 94-95
  secondary schools, 36, 56-66
  special education, 35
  (*see also* Superintendents, Principals)
Administrative cabinet, 38-40
Administrative specializations, 88
American Association of School Administrators, 16, 29, 30, 31
Anderson, Robert H., 102
Argyris, Chris, 104
Assistant principals, 64-65
Assistant superintendents, 38, 42
Authority:
  boards of education, 19-21
  principals, 31-32, 42-44, 63
  relation to organization, 32-34
  superintendents, 31-32, 91-94
Autoinstructional devices, 69, 102

B

Bailey, Thomas D., 83
Bestor, Arthur, 84
Blake, Howard V., 72
Boards of education:
  committees, 23-24
  functions, 19-21, 25-26
  historical development, 18-19
  improvement, 27-28
  legal status, 19-20
  meetings, 24-25
  officers, 22-23
  operation, 24-27
  organization, 22-24
  powers and functions, 19-21, 25-26
  qualifications and characteristics of members, 22, 28

Boards of education (*Cont.*)
  relation to public, 24-25, 26-27
  selection and appointment of members, 22
Bureaucracy in organization, 90

C

Campbell, Roald F., 32
Castetter, William B., 91
Centralized organization, 97
Citizens committees on education, 27, 40-41
City school districts, 7-8, 10-12
Clark, David L., 33
Class size, 71-73
Committee for the Advancement of School Administration, 30-31
Committees:
  board of education, 23-24
  citizens, 27, 40-41
  faculty, 43, 65-66
Common school districts, 7
Conant, James B., 9, 57-58
Consolidation of schools, 8-17 (*see also* Reorganization of school districts)
Cooperative Program in Educational Administration, 30
County school units, 5-6
Courts' interpretation of authority over education, 3, 12, 20

D

Dalton plan, 68, 77
Decentralized organization, 97
Decision-making and organization, 33-34, 104
Department chairmen, 65
Departmentalization, 75-77
DeRemer, Richard W., 102-103
Detroit plan, 77
Districts, 1-17, 83-84, 87-88 (*see also* School Districts)
Dual progress plan, 70-71

E

Education:
  administration of programs, 38, 41-43
  boards of (*see* Boards of education)

111